Najda in Line

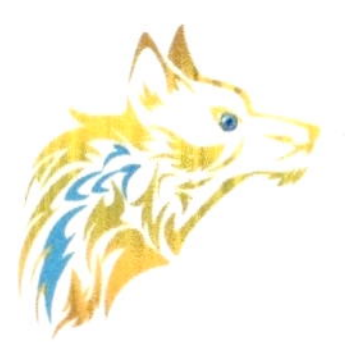

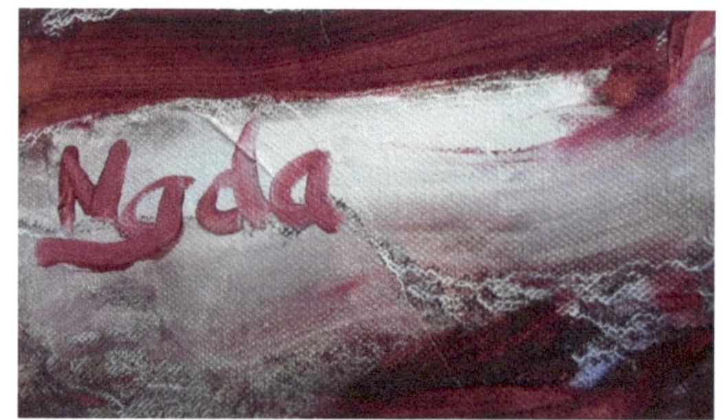

On the cover:
"ELENA WITH HORSE"

*** * ***

Layout Cover and Internal by: Wolf Graham

ISBN 978-1-911424-73-4

Publishing Company:
Black Wolf Edition & Publishing Ltd.
Scotland (UK)
www.blackwolfedition.com

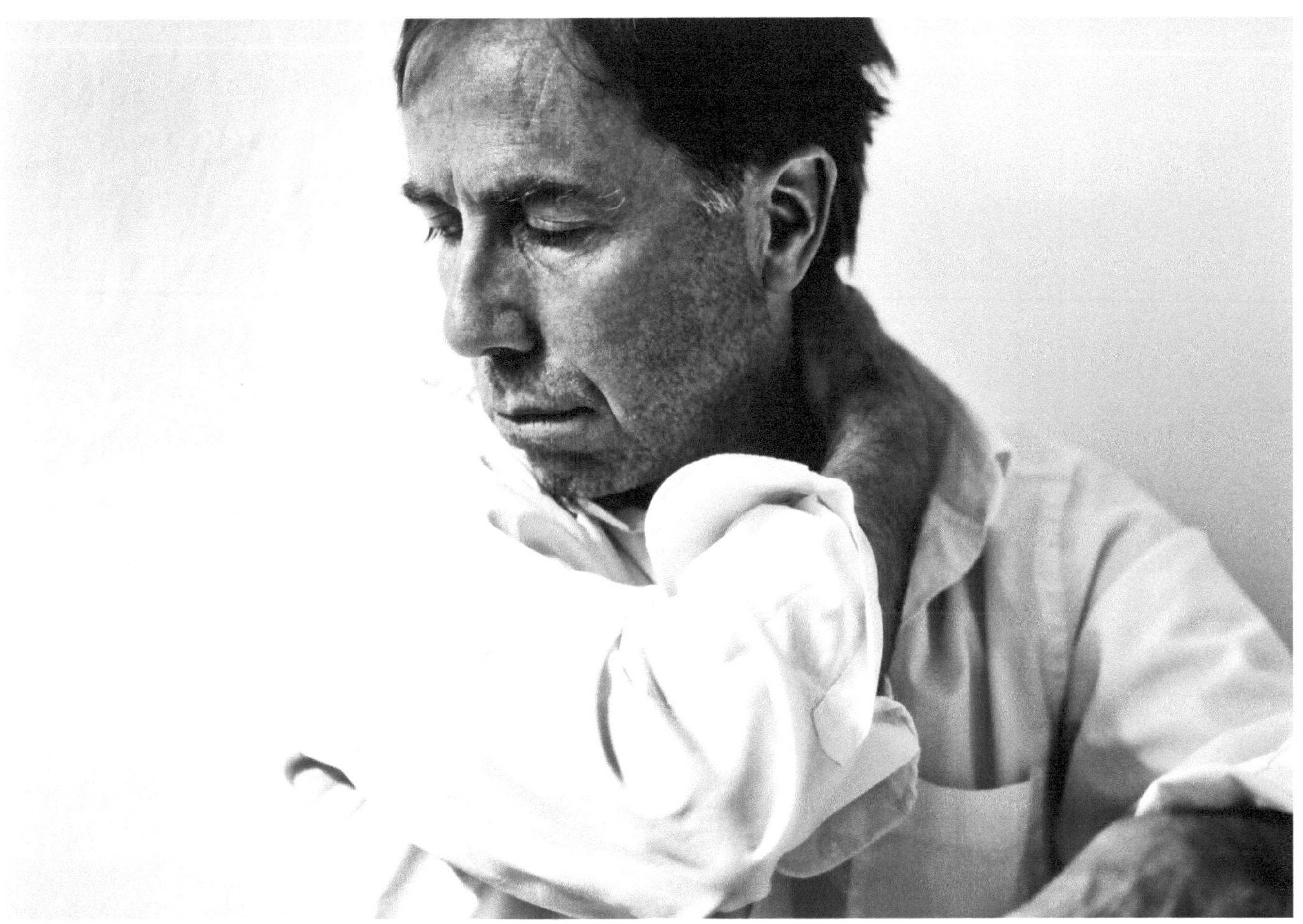

Stephen Najda was born in a Glasgow tenement of Scottish-Polish parentage. The Scottish mountains were an early lure. Since then, Stephen has climbed extensively in the wilderness mountain areas of Europe, the Middle-East, Africa, Asia and the Americas.

Stephen graduated with a PhD in physics from St. Andrews University. Followed by research posts in physics at Tokyo University, CNRS Grenoble and Oxford. Stephen returned to Glasgow to work with a photonics high-tech company and has been 're-born' in Poland with another high-tech venture.

Stephen discovered art by chance and good fortune, pre-empting a 'new path' of discovery and self-expression. Najda's art spans the complete spectrum of human emotion from simple beauty of sensual curvaceous women; through captured moments from the artist's travels; through a wide range of scientific, social, political, philosophical and intellectual questions and debates; to the provocative and challenging brutal reality of war, disease and human tragedy. These theoretical concepts are brought into focus to create a unique visual experience. The art is both, wonderful and enlightening, pleasurable and challenging, beautiful and harrowing, complex and terrifying, producing powerfully evocative images that are entirely relevant to the modern world and questioning our path into the future.

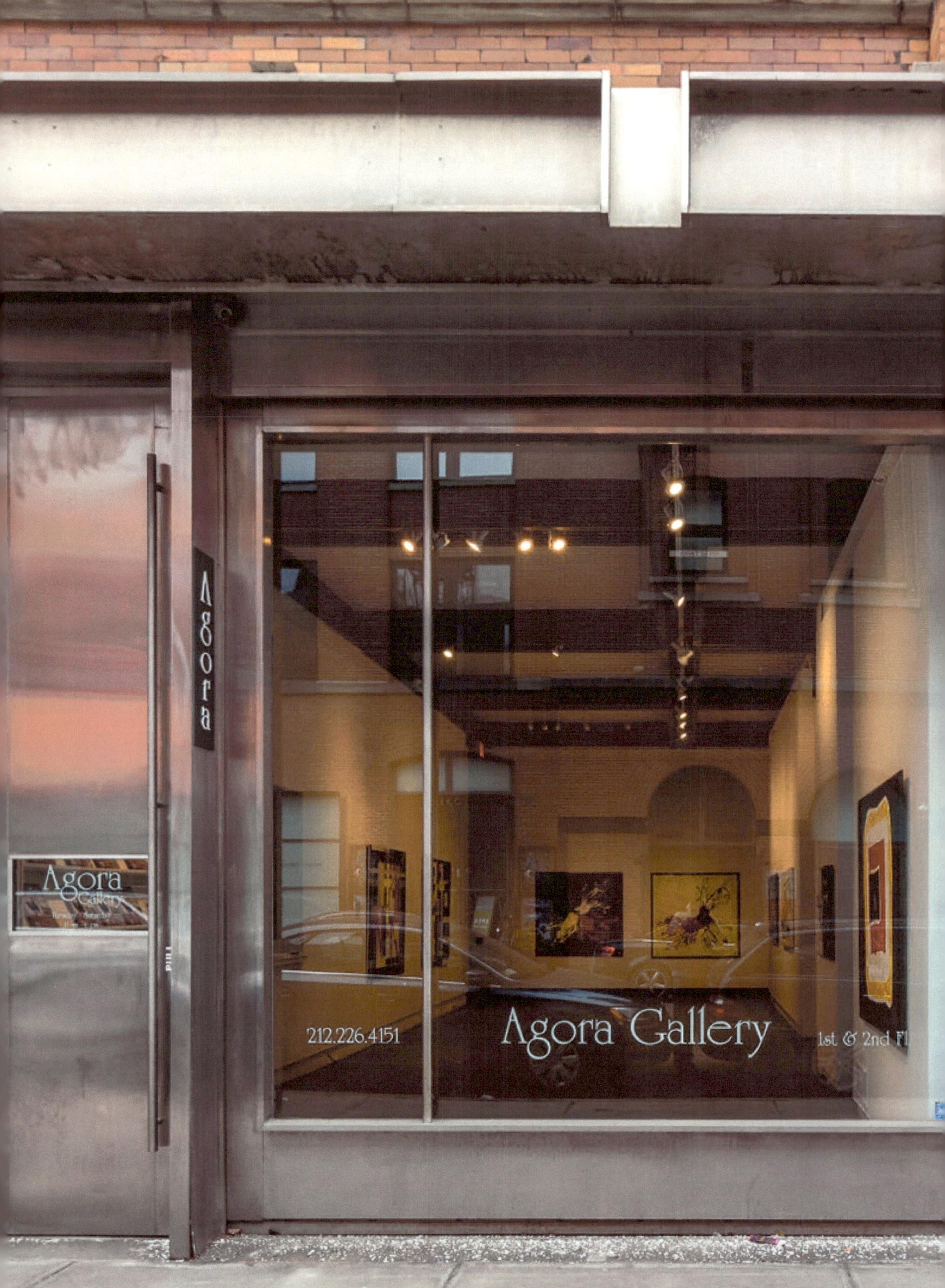

Agora
Agora Gallery
212.226.4151
Agora Gallery
1st & 2nd Fl

Najda in Line: a series of drawings by Stephen Najda

Stephen Najda is a precociously talented and prolific artist more commonly known for big, bold, hugely imaginative paintings, very much in the style of Picasso-Matisse-De Kooning.
Najda in Line explores a different aspect of the artist, the simplicity and beauty of pencil or pen on paper.

Drawing is the ultimate discipline, everything is stripped bare, offering a glimpse into the fundamental, raw imagination of the artist. Najda creates powerful and expressive drawings that are as enigmatic and individualistic as the artist himself. Every mark is explicitly recorded, indelibly capturing the moment in the artists ephemeral mind. Pure emotion flows through the line with a musical sense of time and rhythm to create an 'art harmony' of purity of thought. One can feel the freedom and joy, the simplicity and spontaneity of expression. This is a personal conversation with the artist.

Najda captures his 'primitive-self', exploring the space between imagination and dream to produce an 'abstraction of thought', bringing a unique vision of spontaneity and emotion. 'I draw what arrives in my imagination. Where it comes from, I have no idea. That is the adventure'. You can feel Najda's mind at work, a graceful movement of hand exploring new ideas, taking risks, deconstructing, and reformulating the image, economic in line, yet powerful in presence. Nothing is removed. Everything is stripped bare to reveal a purity of thought.

Many works by Najda bear a certain qualitative aspect of impenetrability – an ambiguity, allowing the imagination of the viewer to enter into the narrative and explore the abstraction. At first glance one can interpret this as cubism, but Najda would describe this as 'cubism without the cubes'. Najda reduces complexity to simplicity in a highly precise line, and simultaneously does the opposite by creating complexity from simplicity - a Najdaification by morphing an 'expression of thought' – this is a new form of pictorial sign language. 'I draw how I feel, where I am, who I'm drawing, and not according to anatomy, rationale or reason'. For Najda, drawing is an autonomous equal to painting rather than a preparatory exercise.

The work is characterised by a virtuosity use of line, meticulous studies of nature and the human condition. With Najda, complexity is reduced to simplicity; simplicity is turned to complexity. Realism morphs into abstraction; abstraction morphs into realism. This juxtaposition of ideas, concepts and styles is typical of Najda. Just as you pin down an idea or concept or interpretation, the artist will give you the opposite.

Najda is an artist with an interest in everything, the subject matter is boundless. 'Najda in Line' is a snap-shot of work covering several years over a wide range of topics, with the human figure central. A confident hand on paper, suddenly turns into an agitated presence morphing into something else enticing the viewer to step into the artwork and be there in the moment. A common thread runs through all his artwork – a bold vision, delineating line and energetic fluidity to produce a powerful narrative.

Some of the most accessible of all Najda's drawings are the classical nudes and reclining odaliques, bathed in a soft imaginary Mediterranean light, speak for themselves. You can feel the hand of an Impressionist, an essence of Matisse, the contours of Cezanne and intense marks of Van Gogh.

At the other extreme are the Gadenenexperiment (German for thought experiments originally devised by the pioneers of quantum physics to explain the mysteries of the sub-atomic world). The Gadenenexperiment or Gadengraffexperiment work are the most difficult to explain. This is drawing from what comes up from the deep. Close your eyes and see what happens. Drawing in line, conventional, changing to random, chaotic line, losing it then bringing it back as a 'thought drawing experiment' – close your eyes and let your imagination take over. These are quick gestural exercises that capture the form and emotion in the most direct expression of the artistic mind. The Gadengraffexperiment work is a deliberate attempt not to allow the mind follow the past, but to force a re-think, a re-calculation, a re-evaluation, as Najda explains 'I like to draw what I don't know'.

Angela Di Bello,
Executive Director
Agora Gallery 530 W 25th St, New York, NY 10001, USA
and Editor-in-Chief of ARTisSpectrum Magazine.

Najda in Line

"Animals"

Agora Gallery

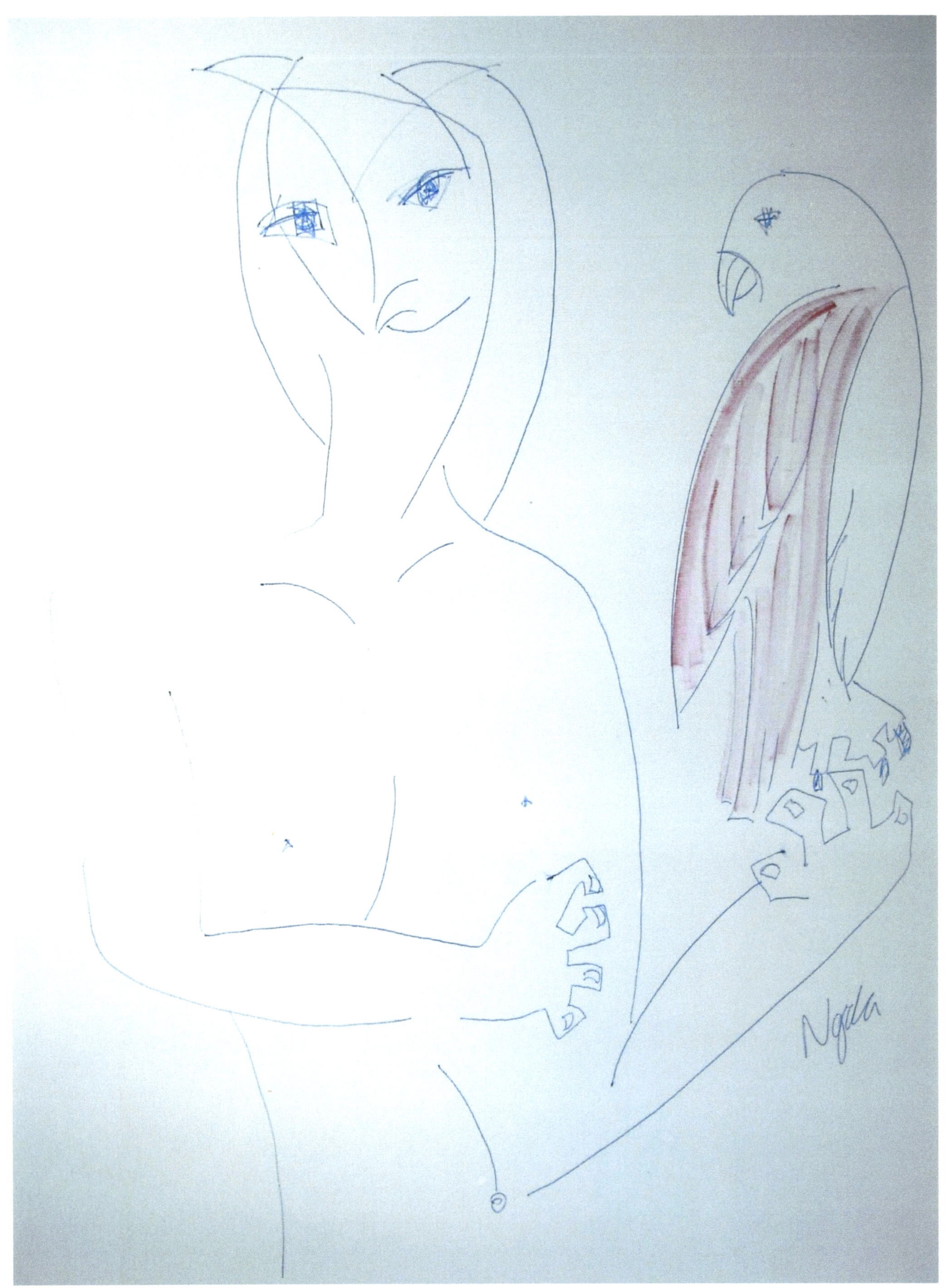

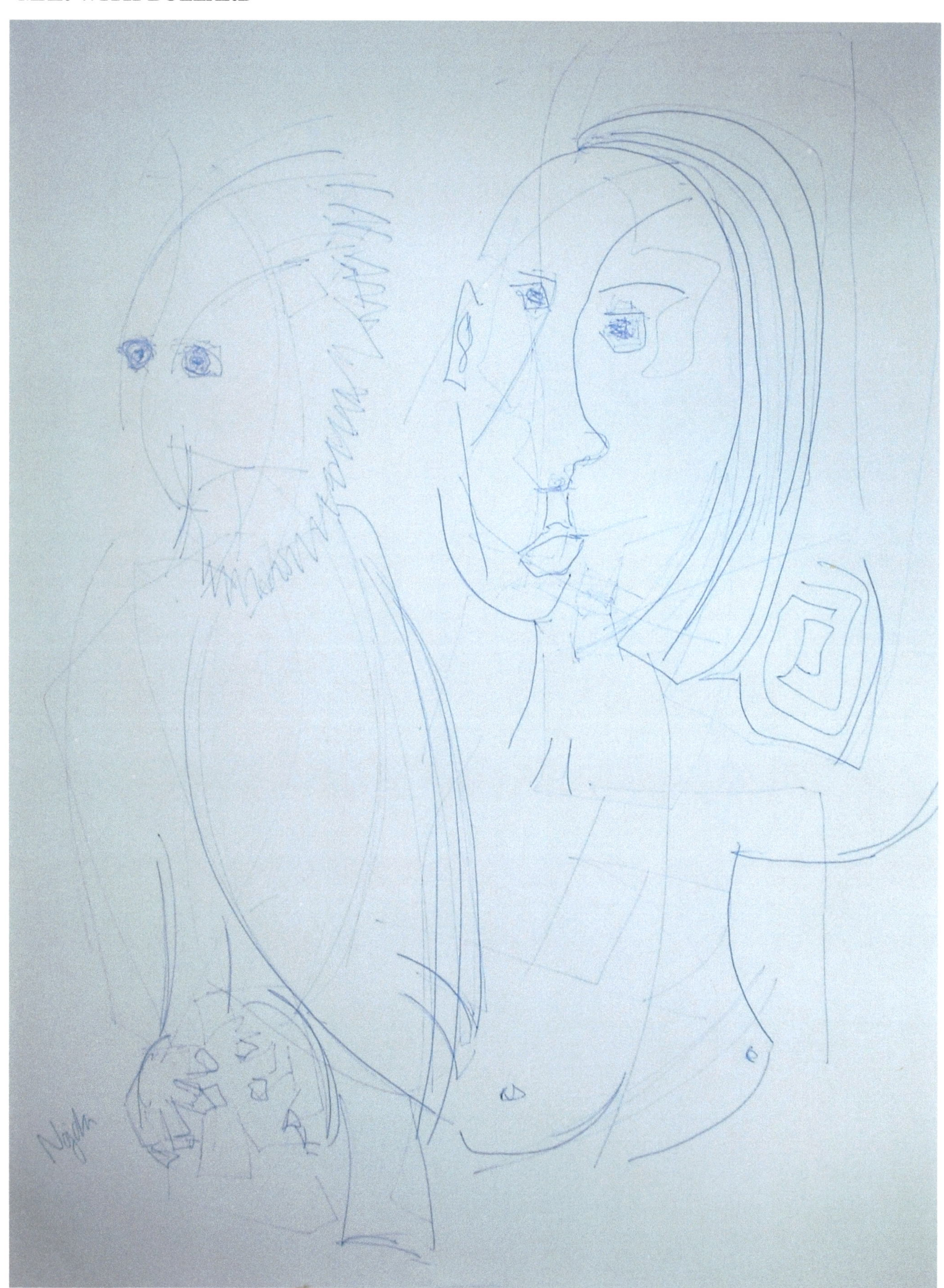

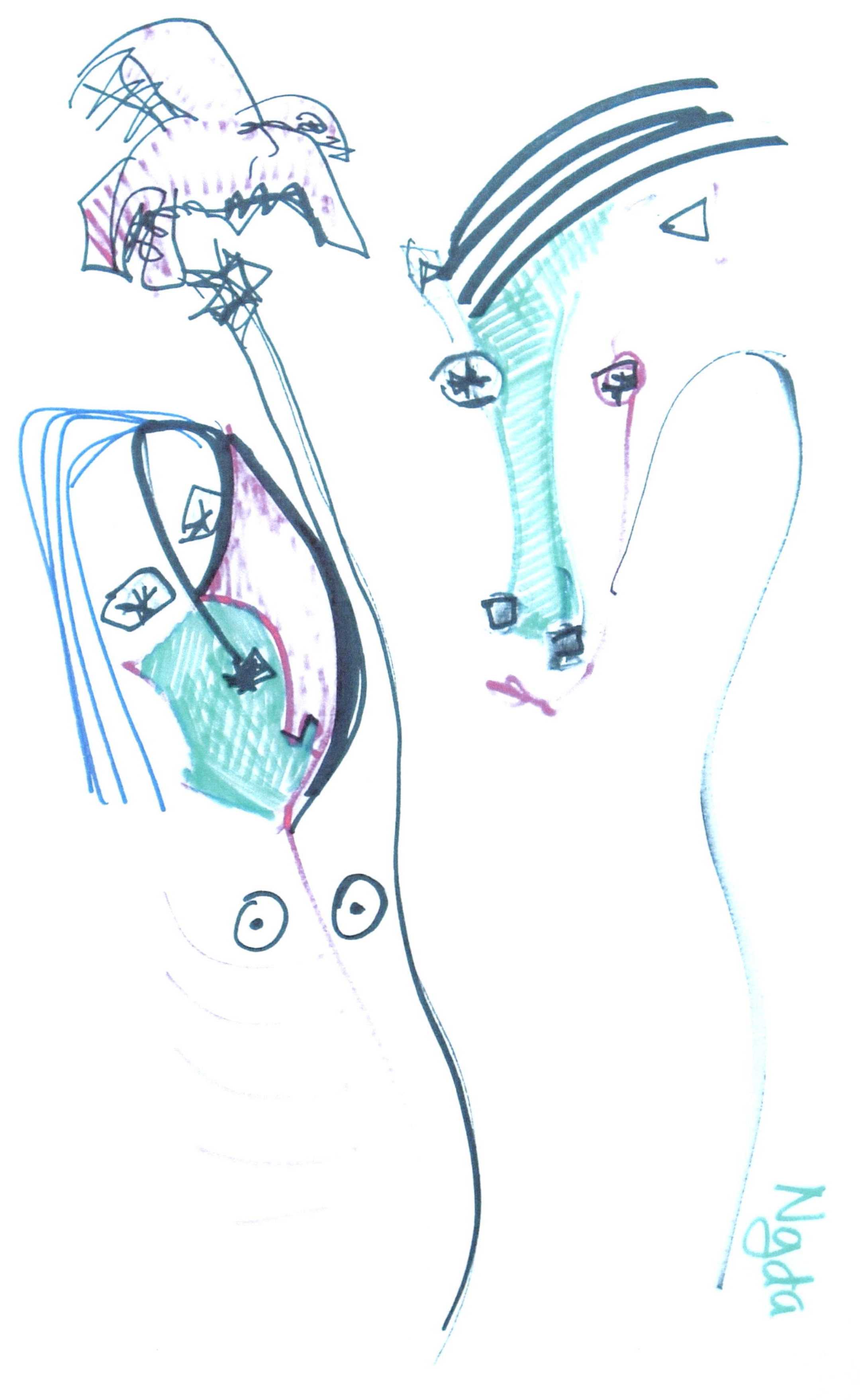

"SLEEPING GIRL AND DOG"

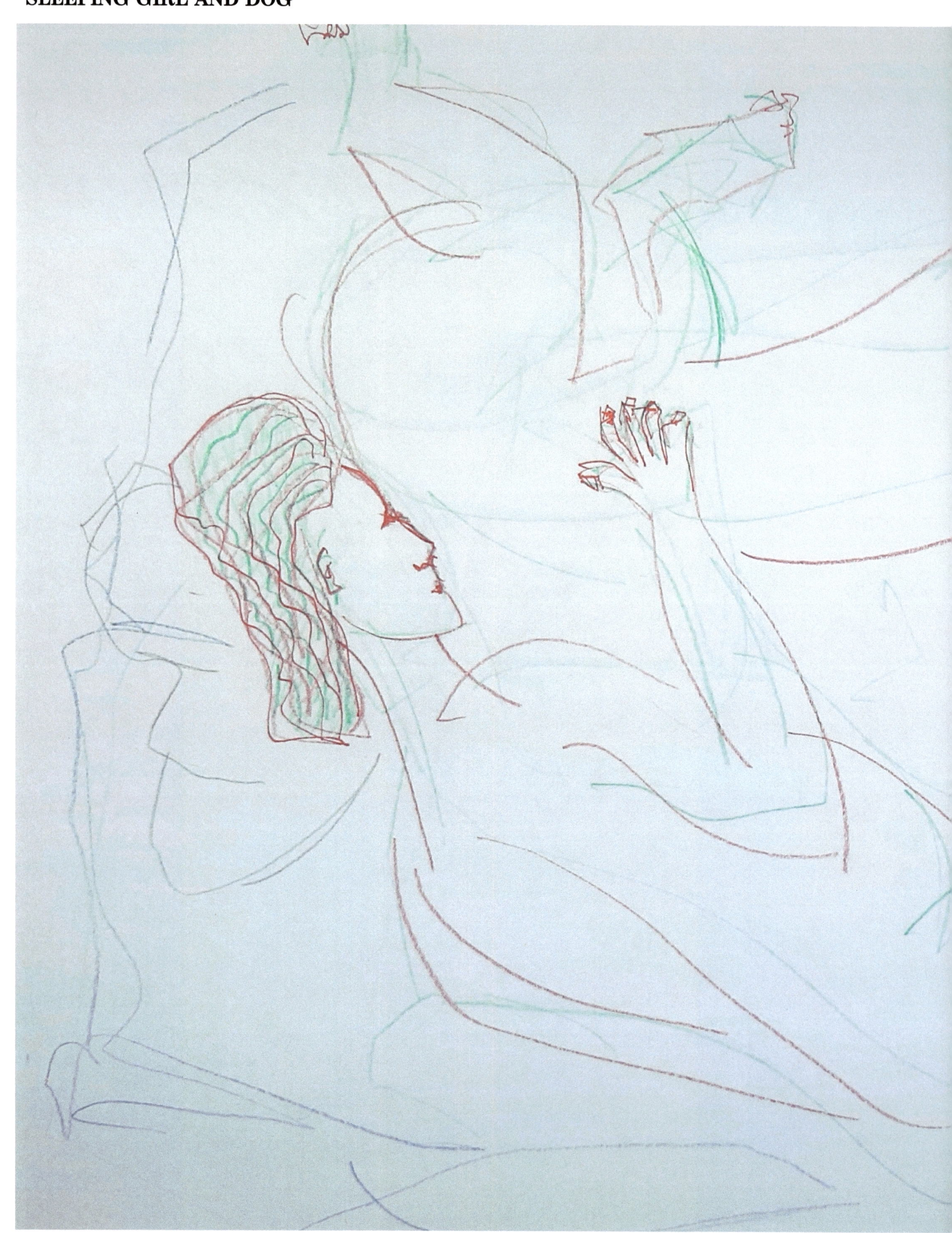

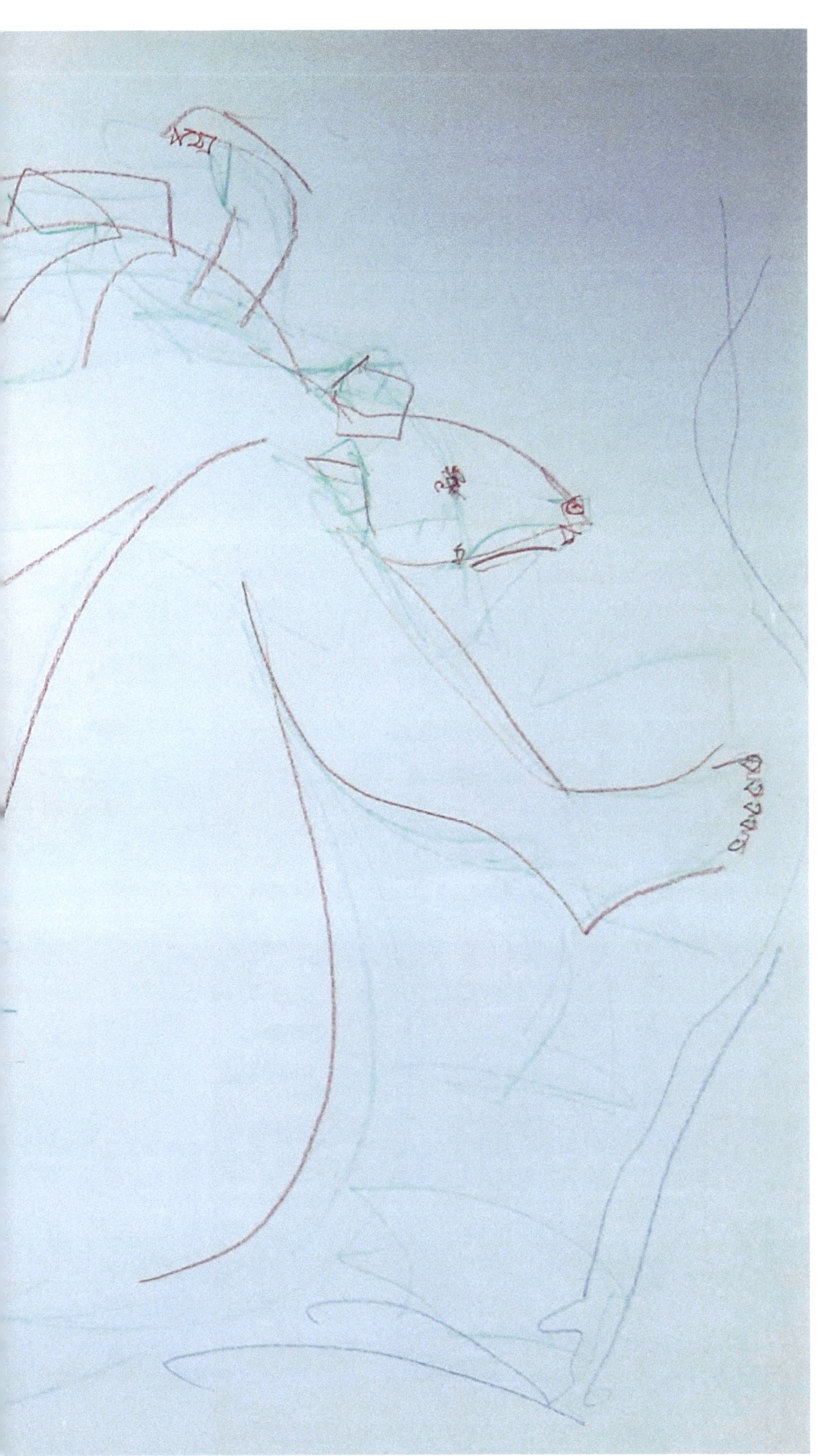

"SLEEPING GIRL AND TWO DOGS"

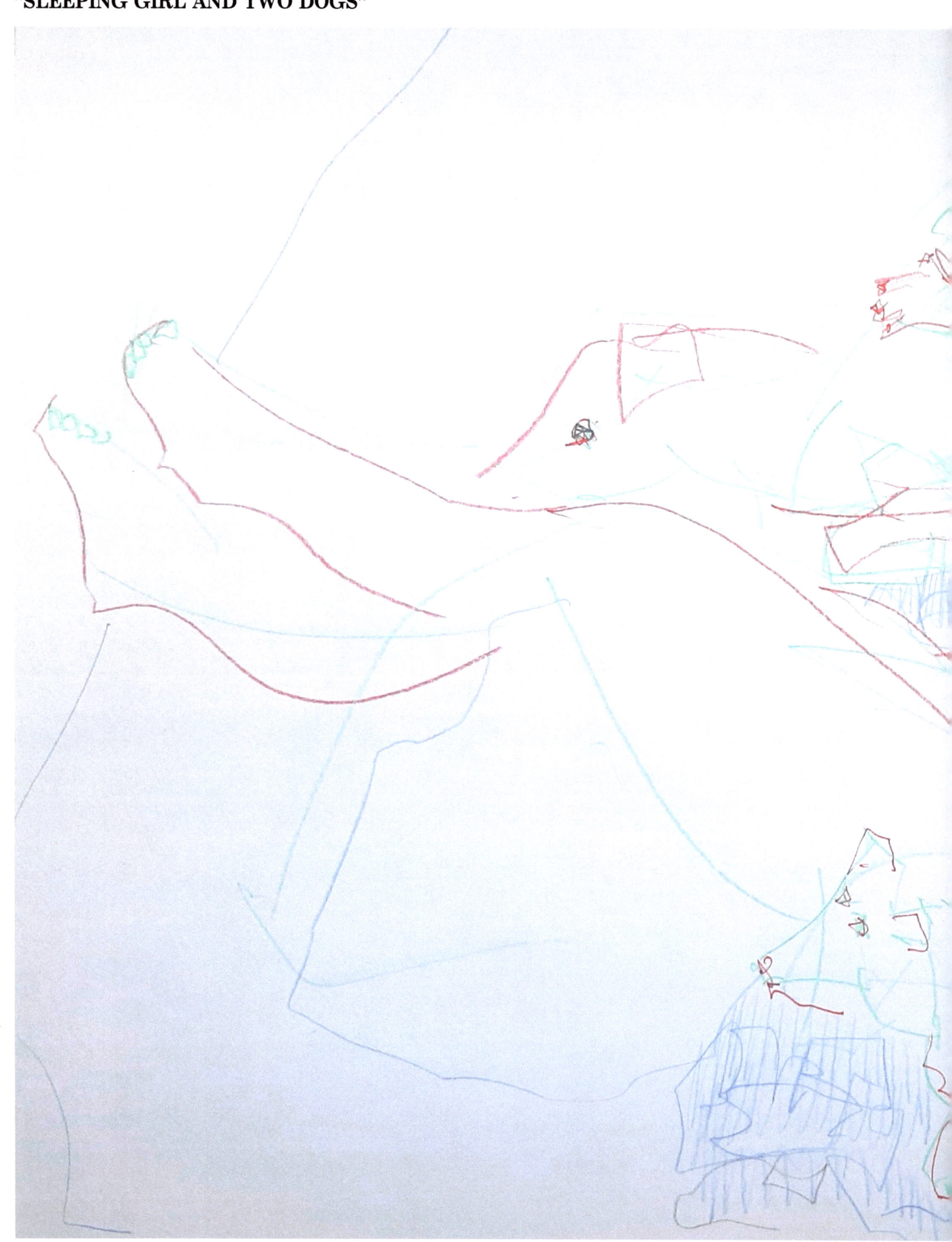

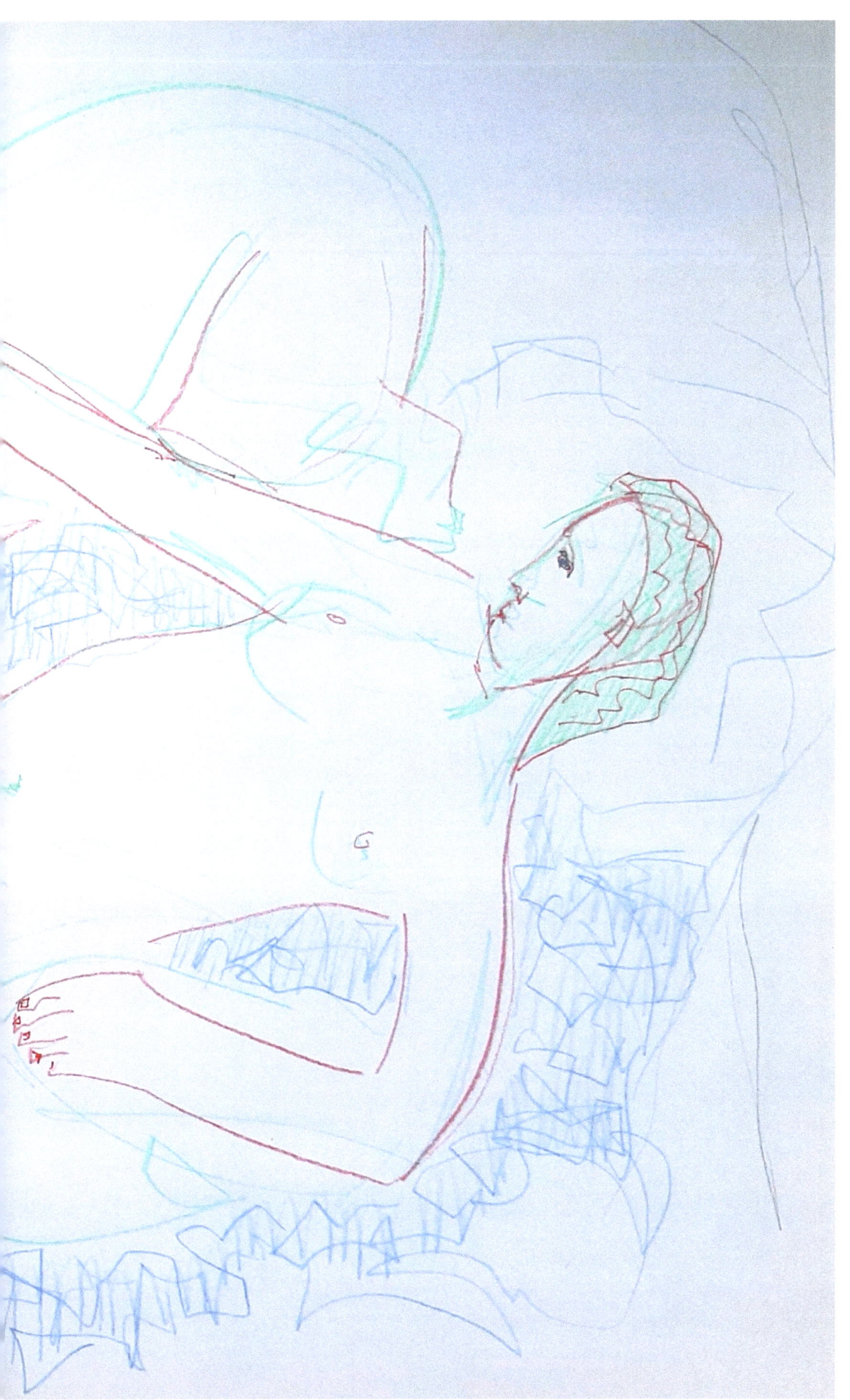

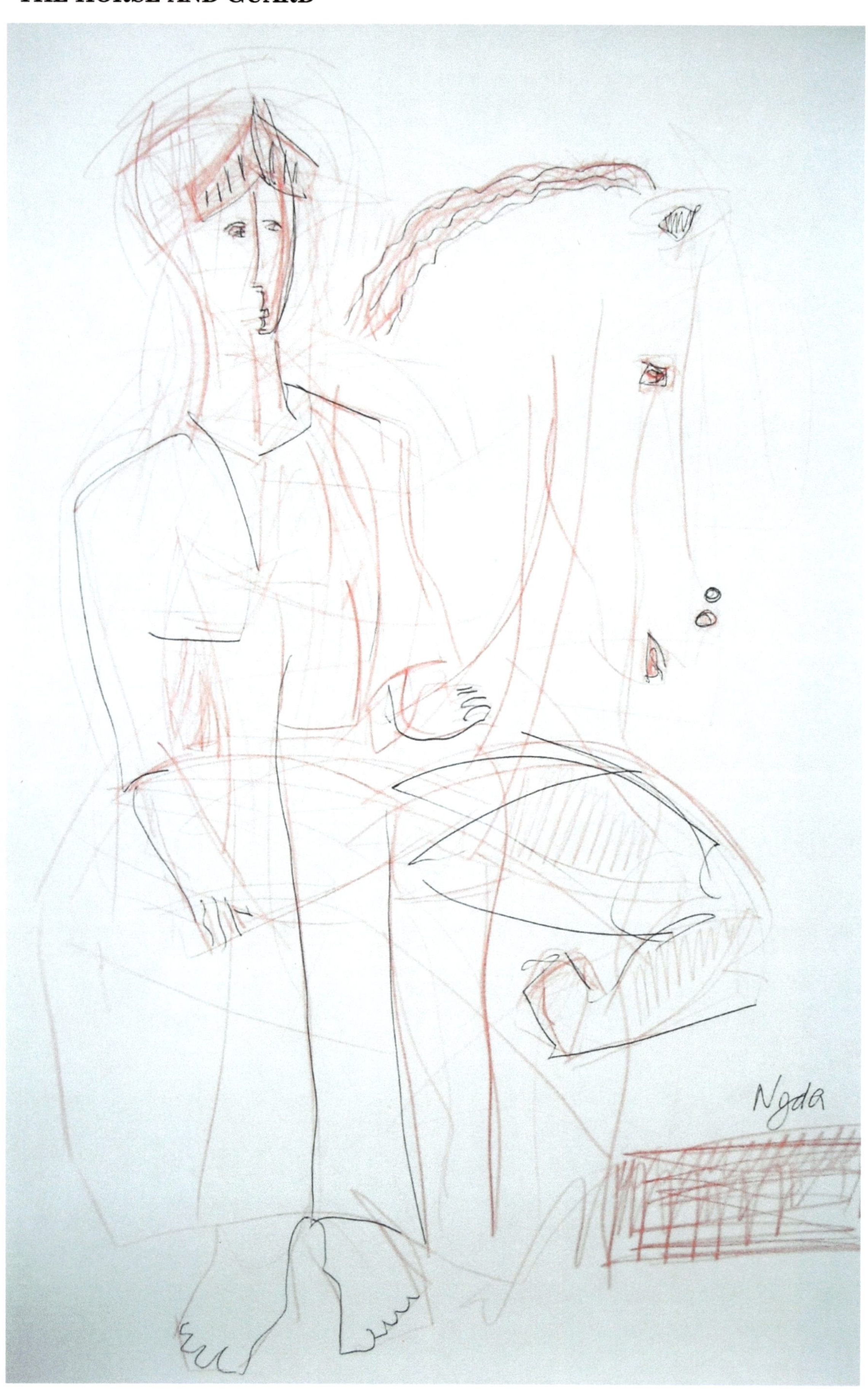

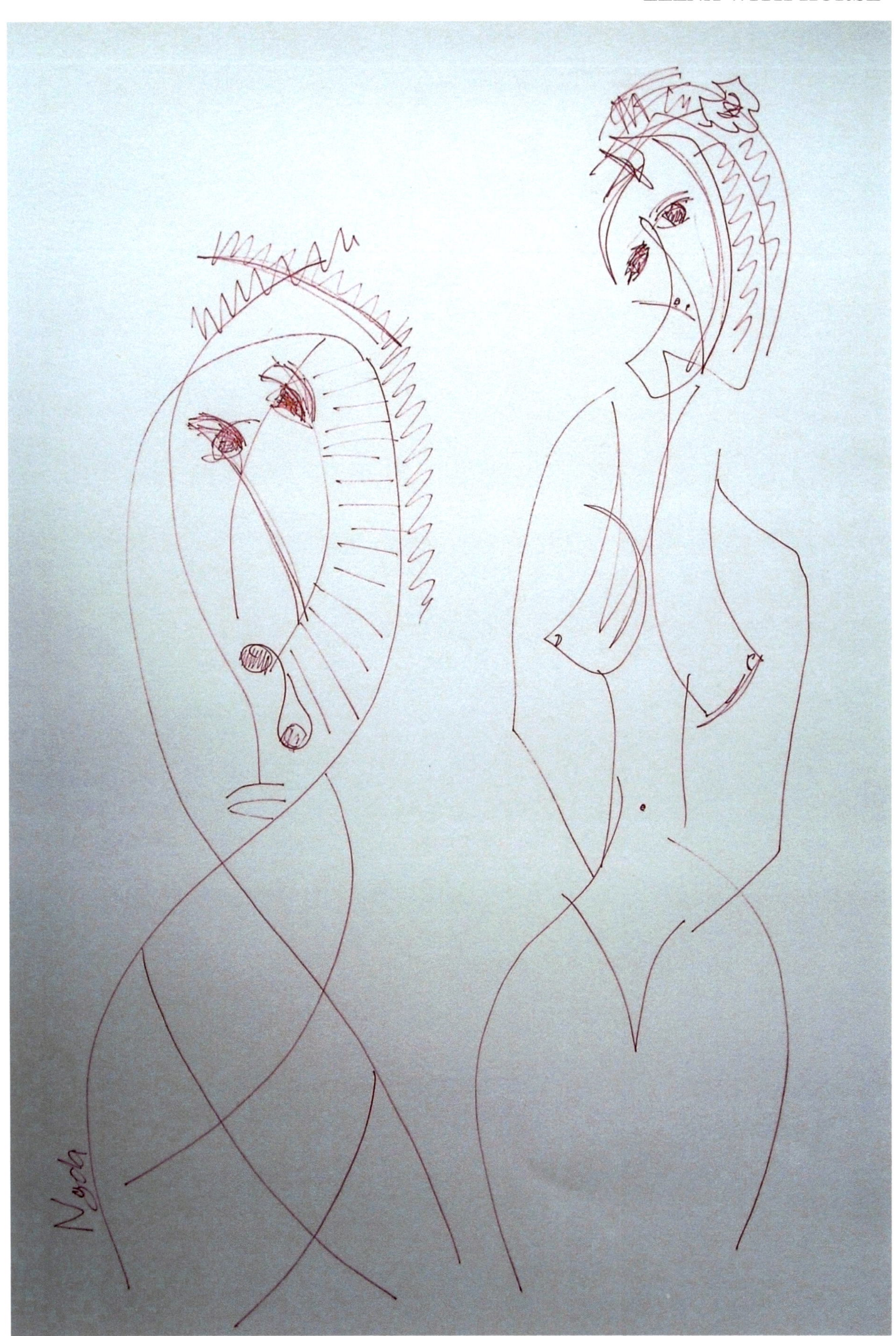

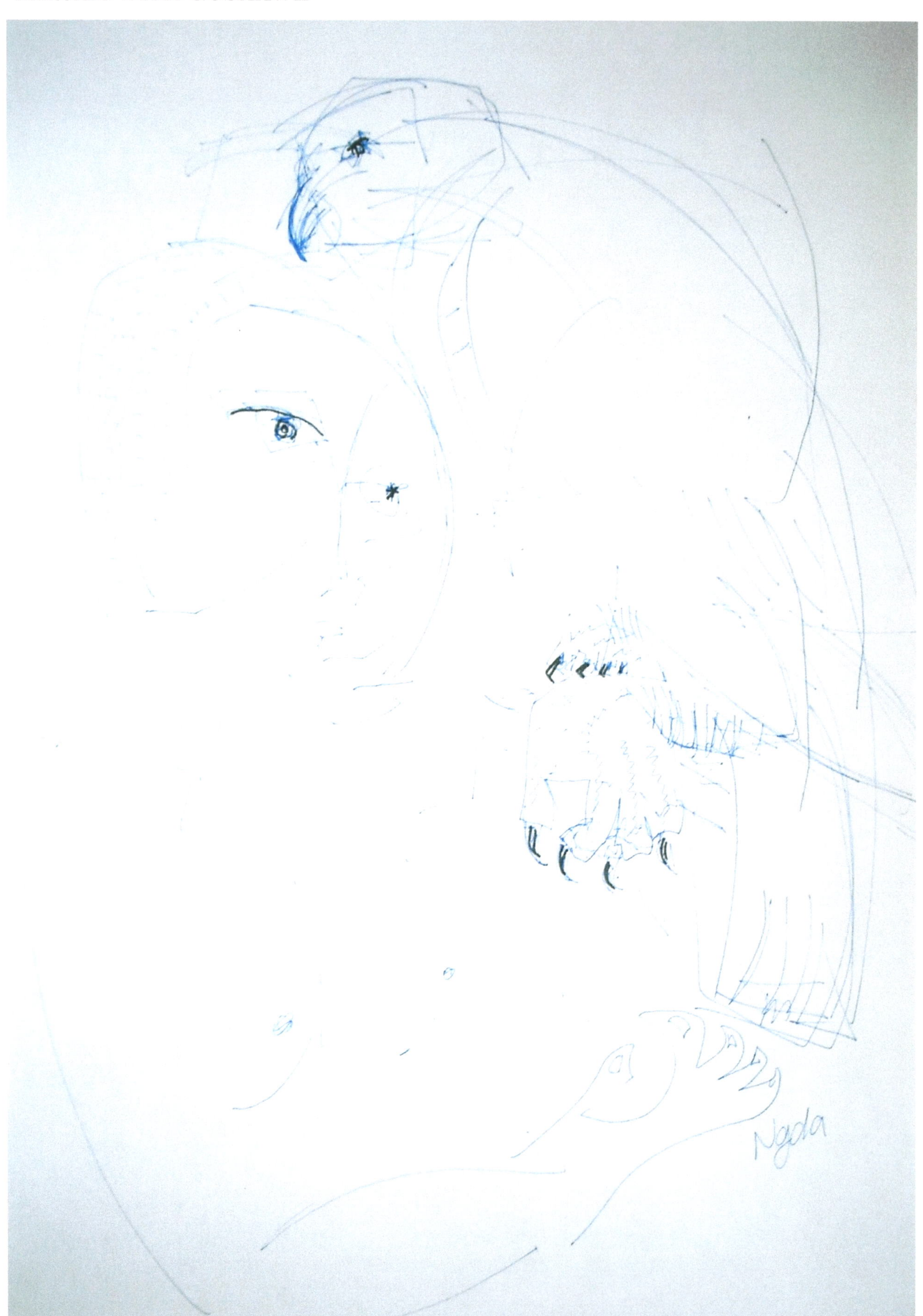

Najda in Line

"Dreams and Reality"

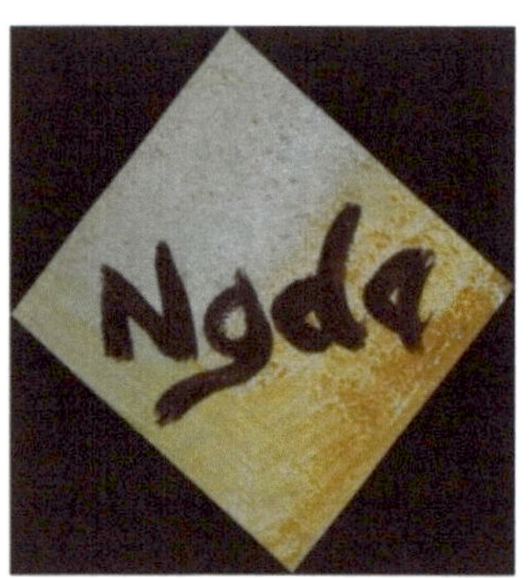
Ngde

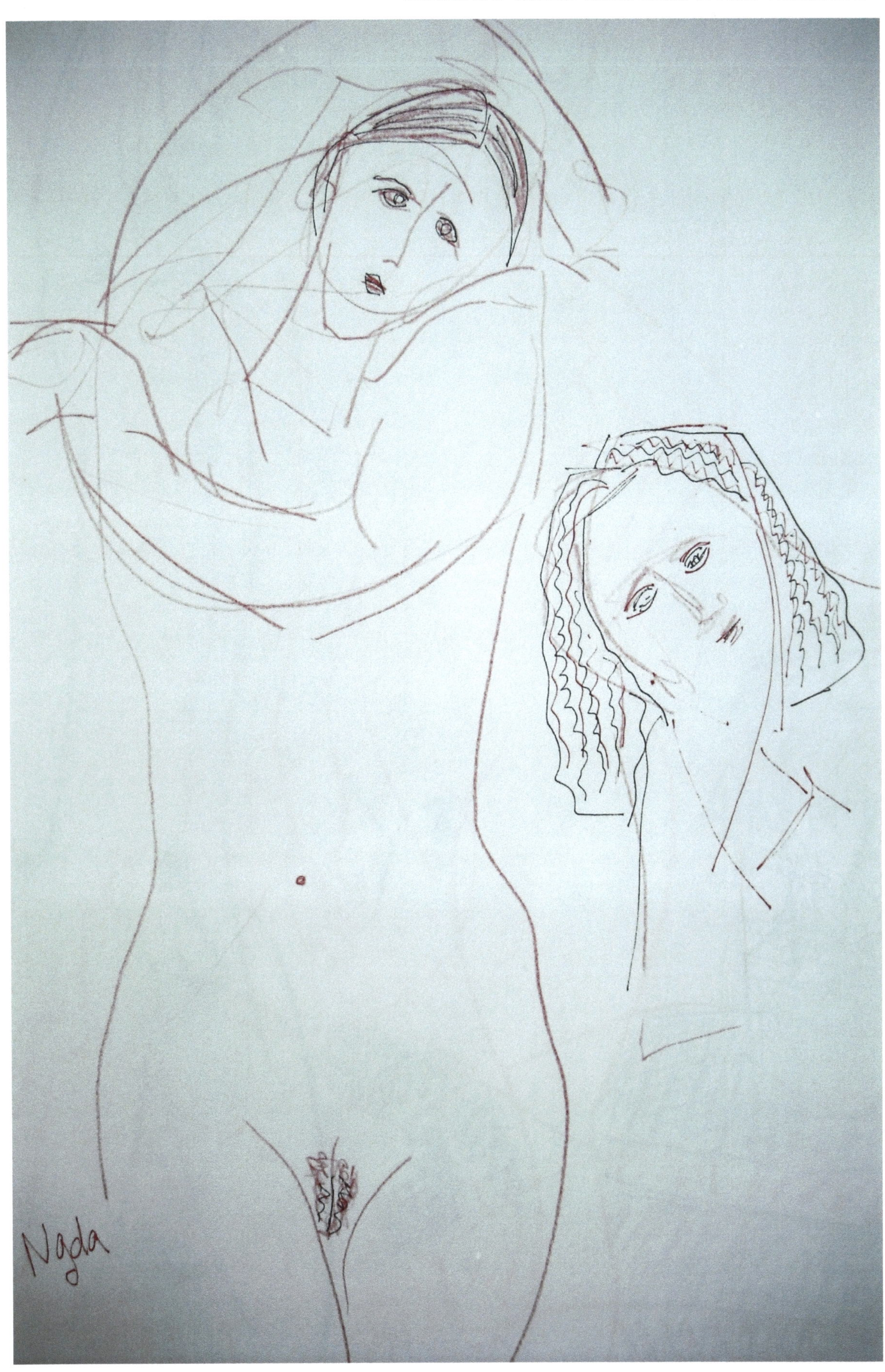

Nada

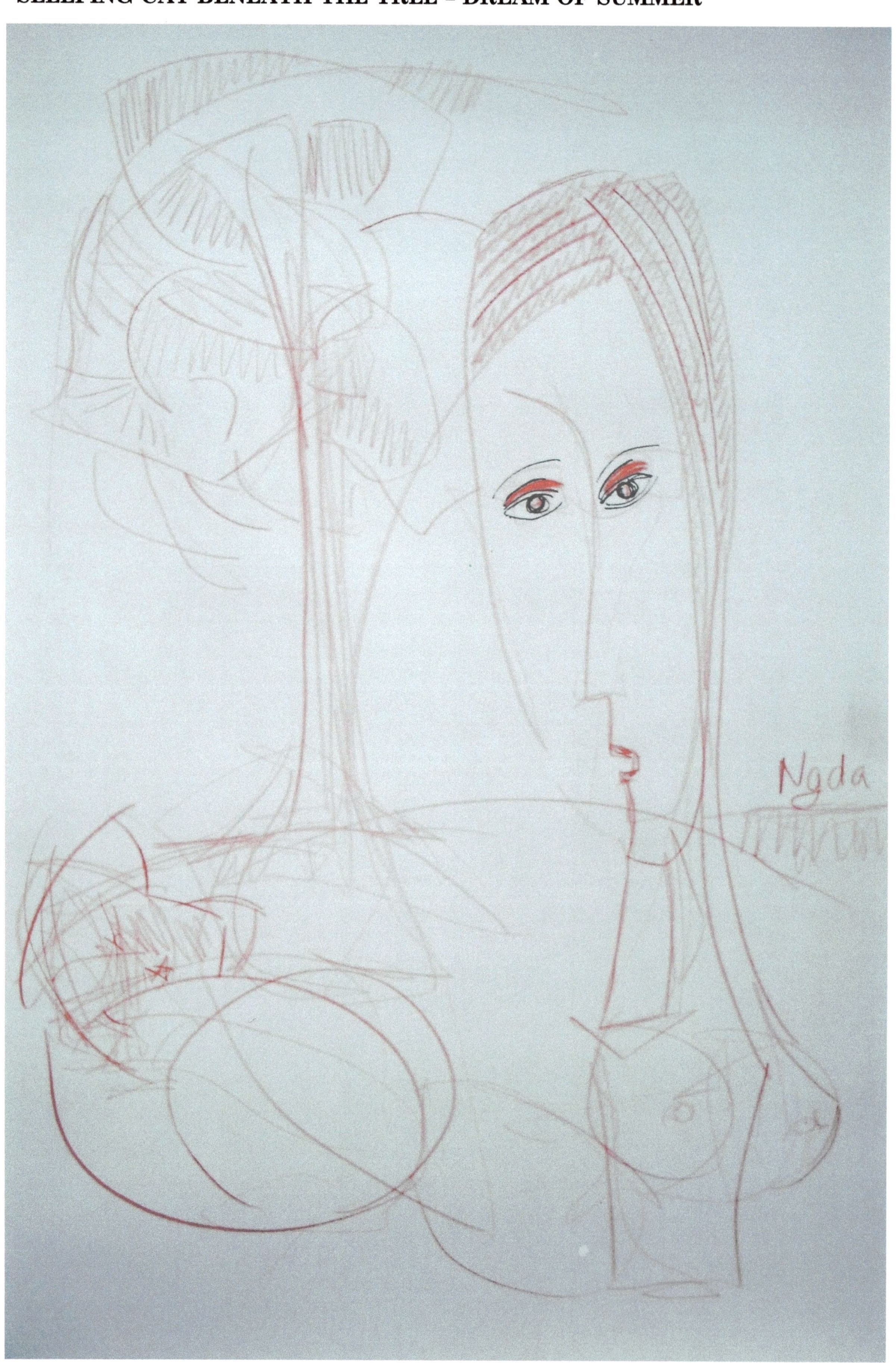

"SLEEPING CAT BENEATH THE TREE – DREAM OF SUMMER"

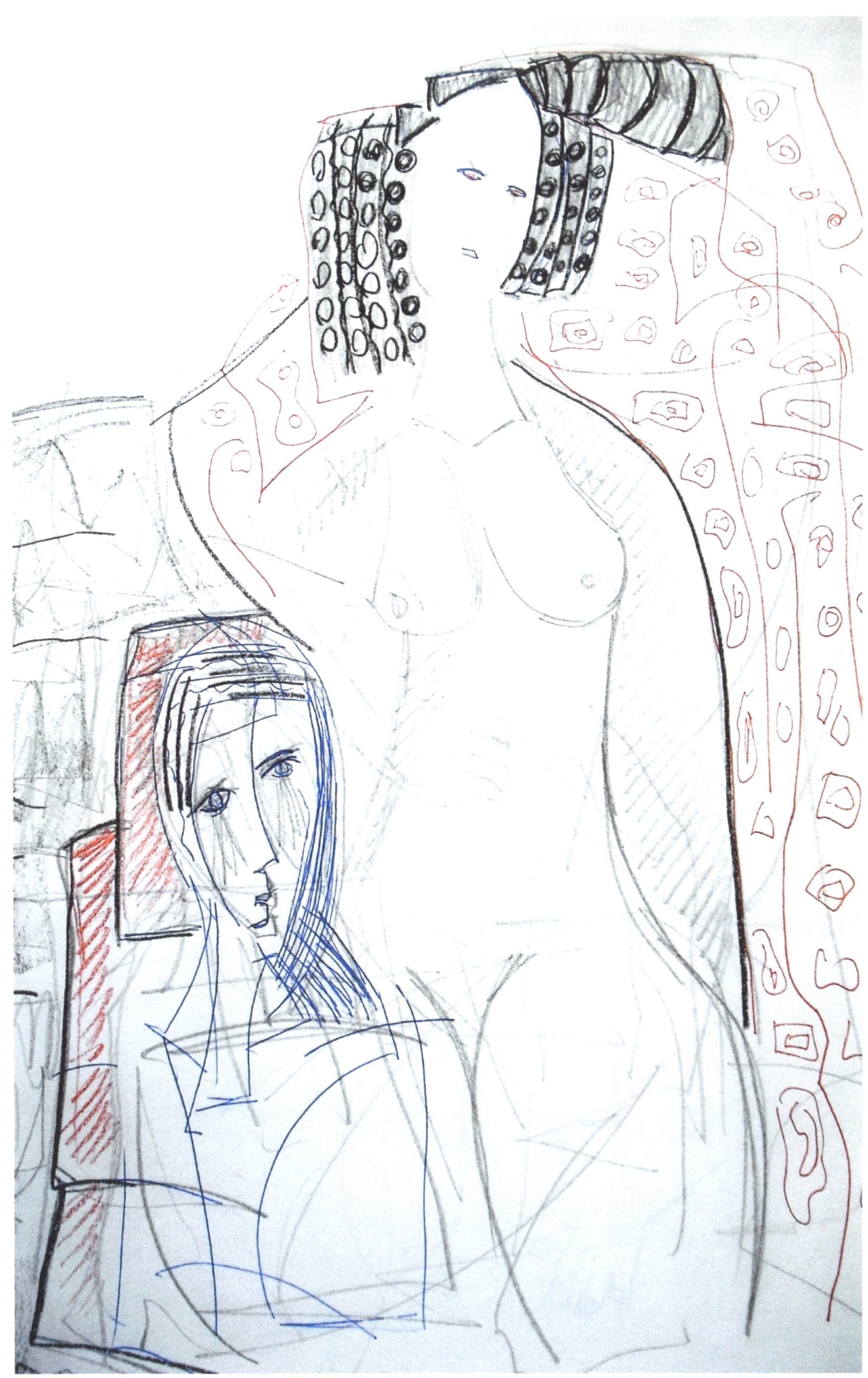

"CONTEMPLATION OF TIME"

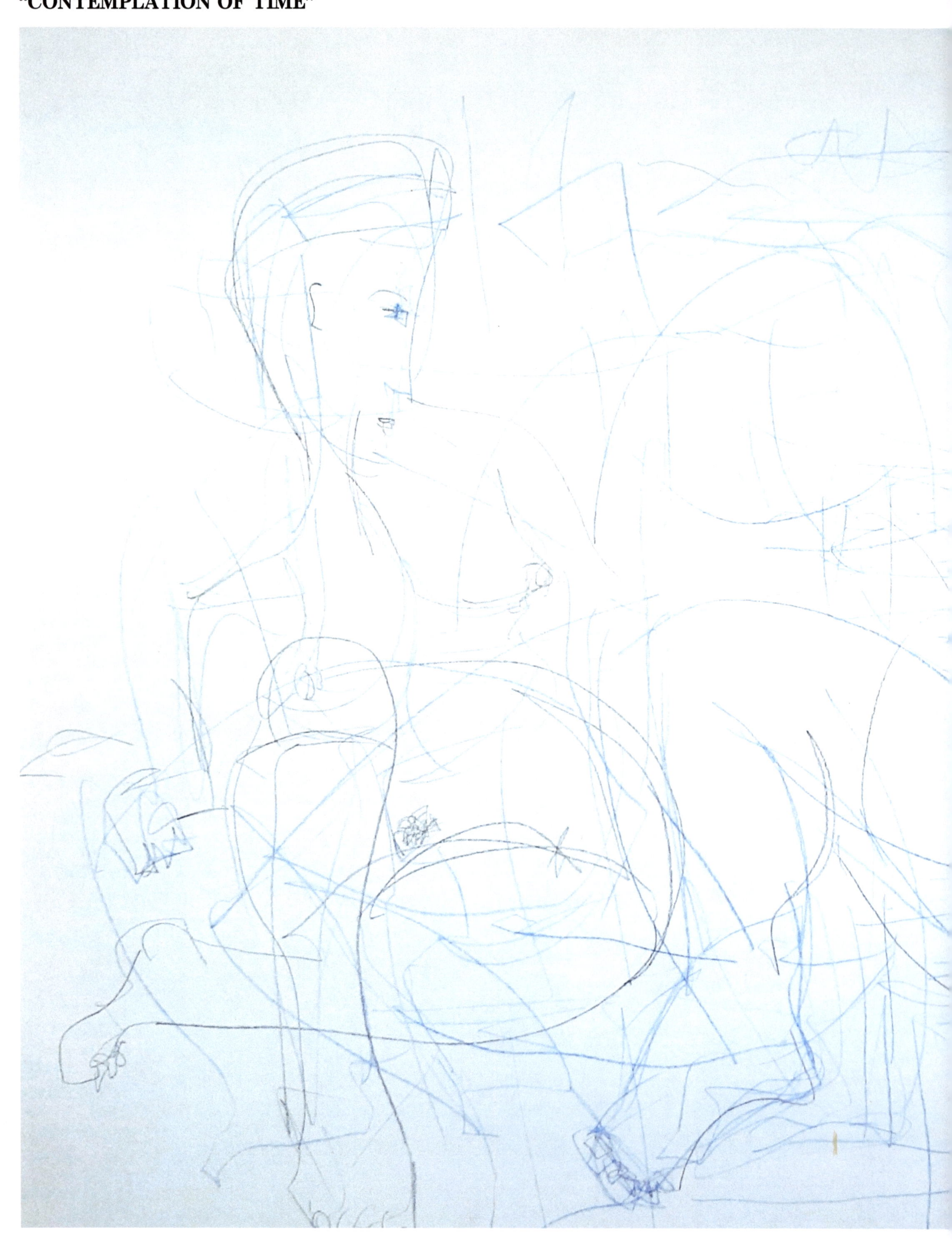

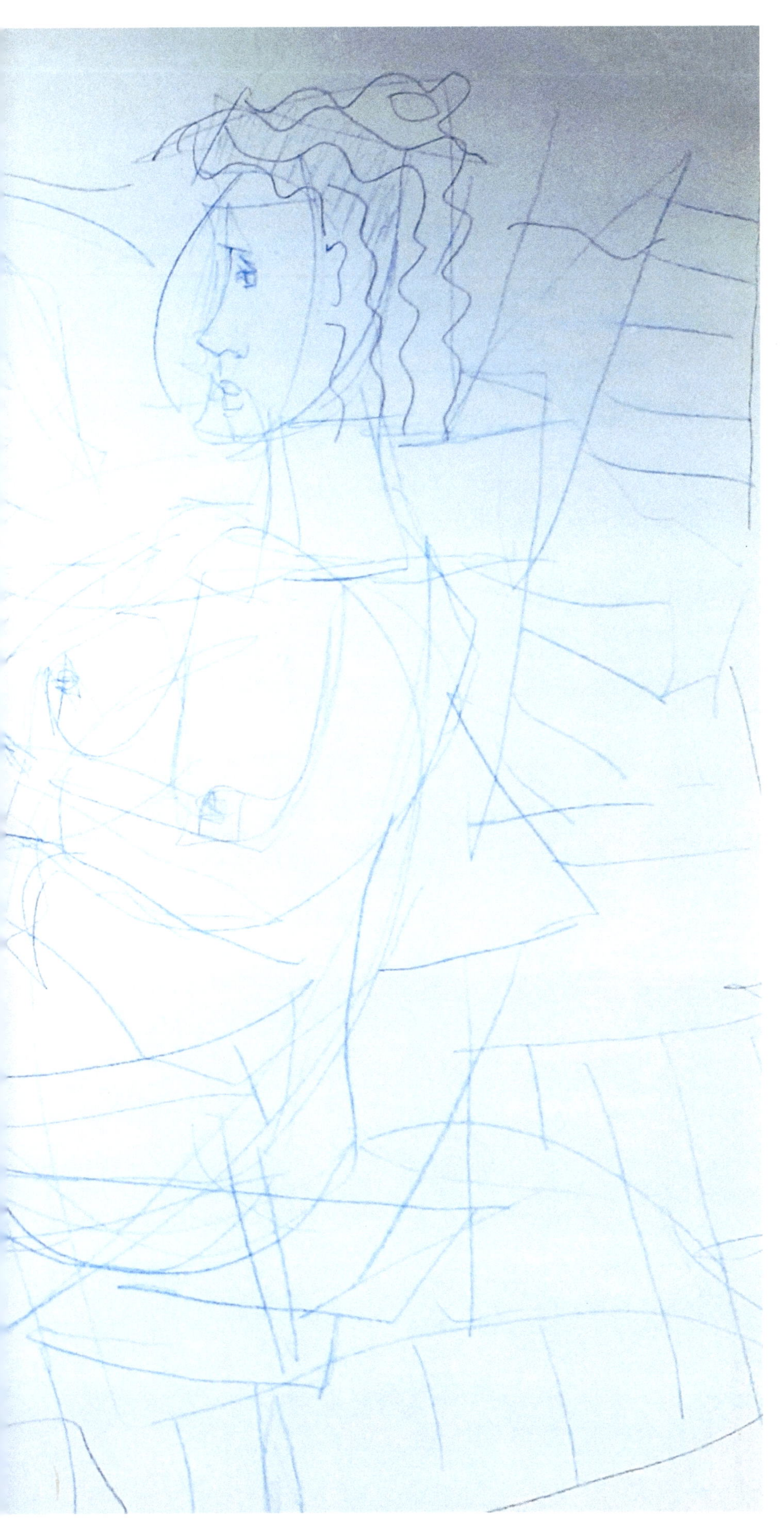

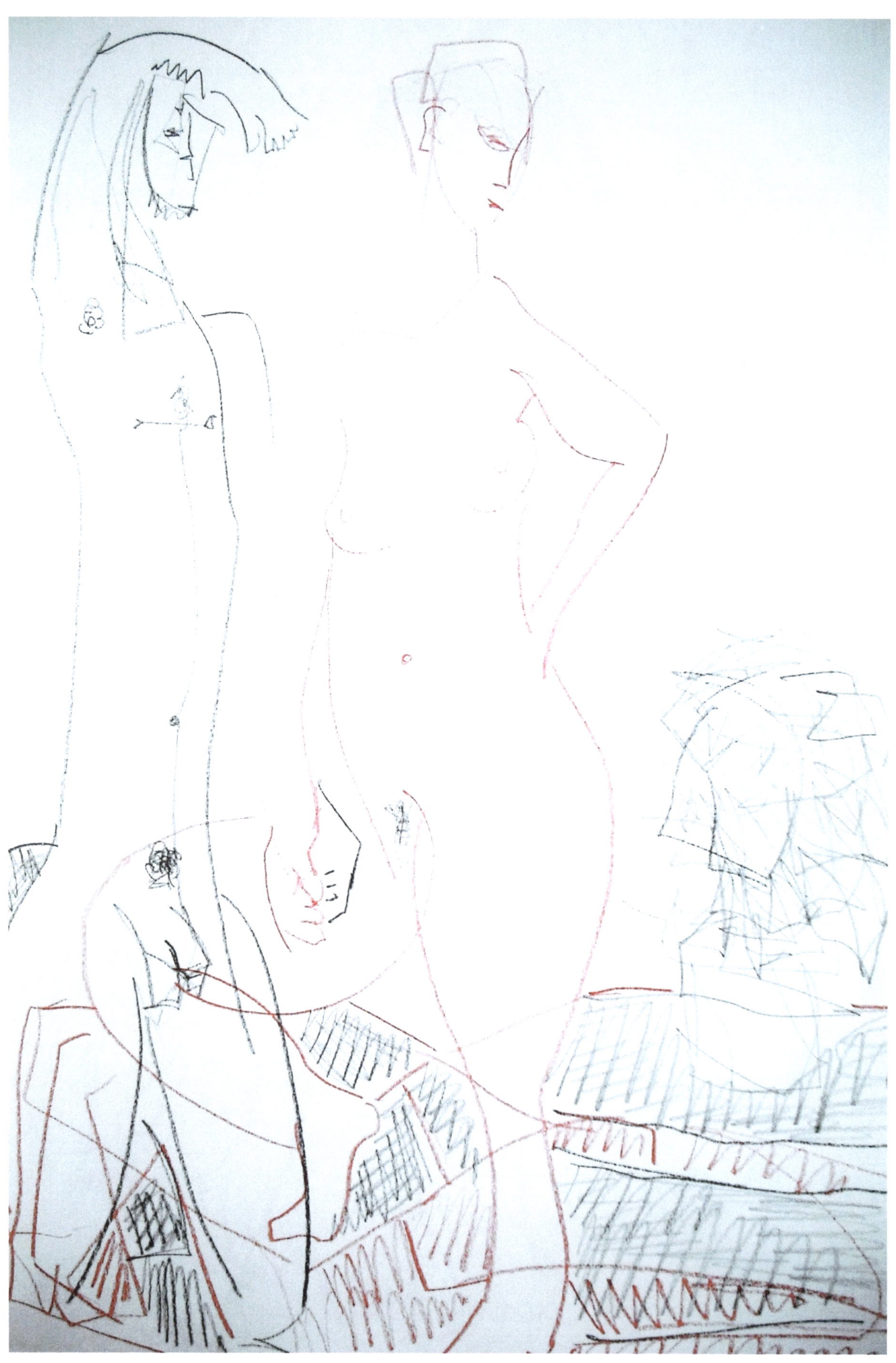

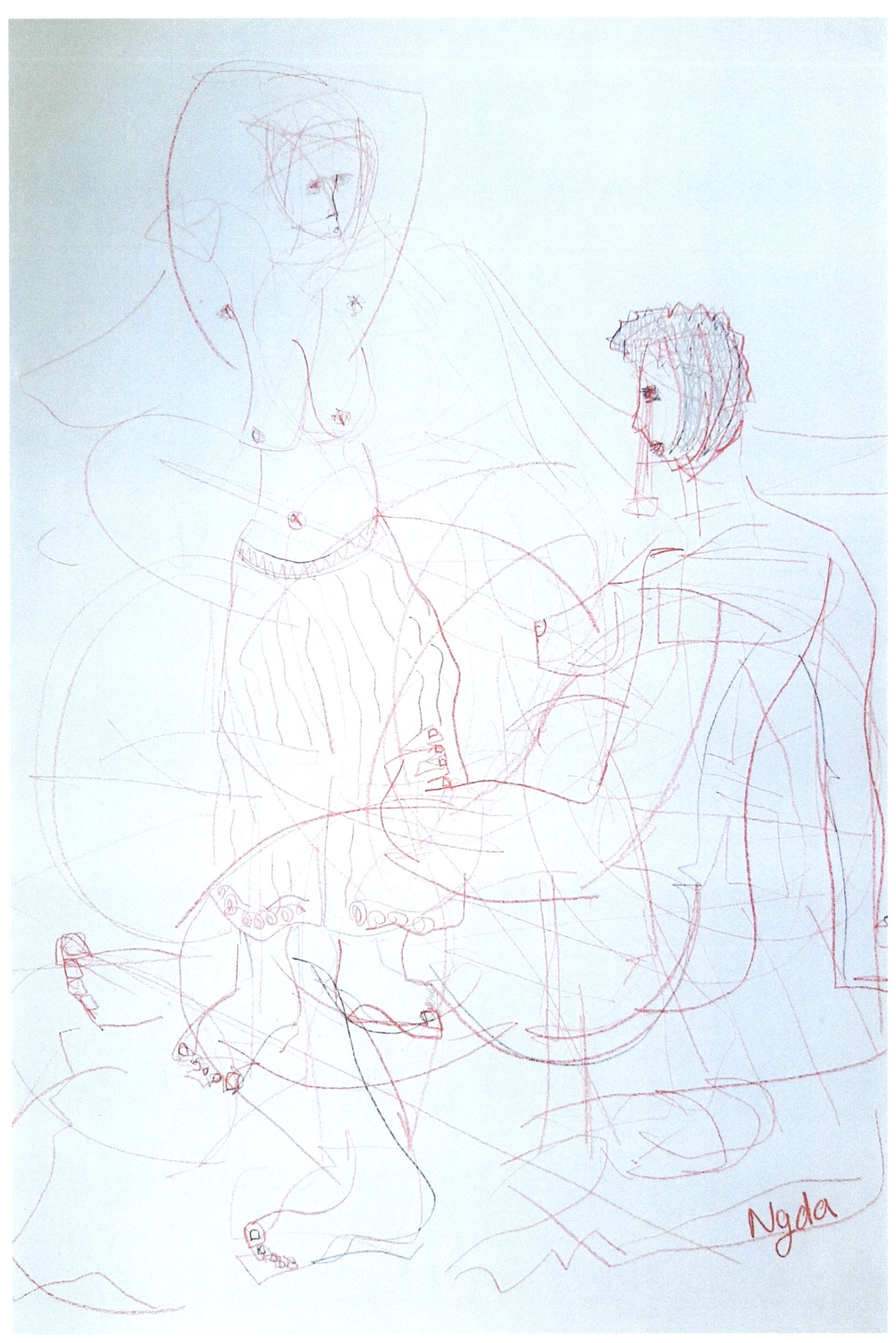
Ngda

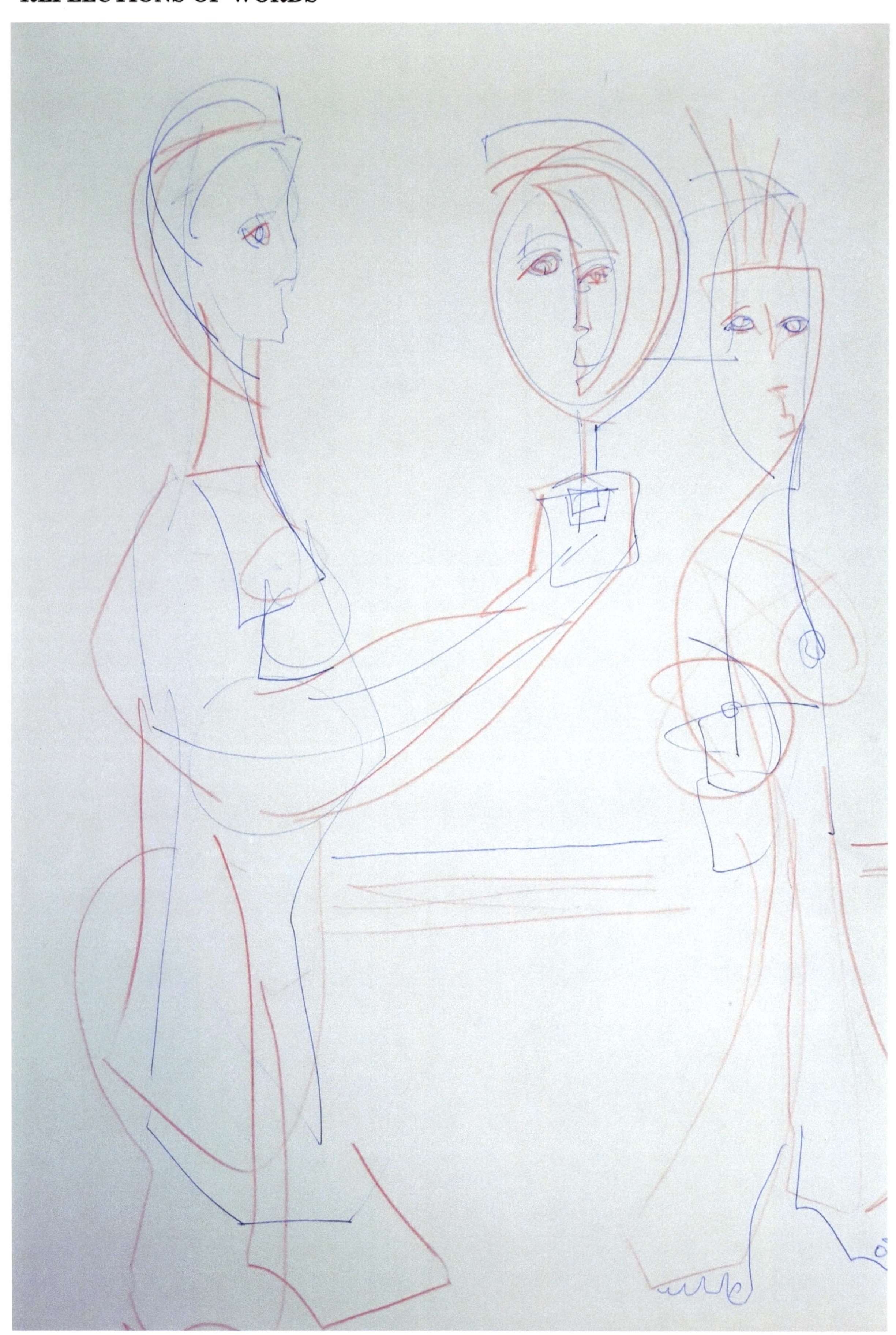

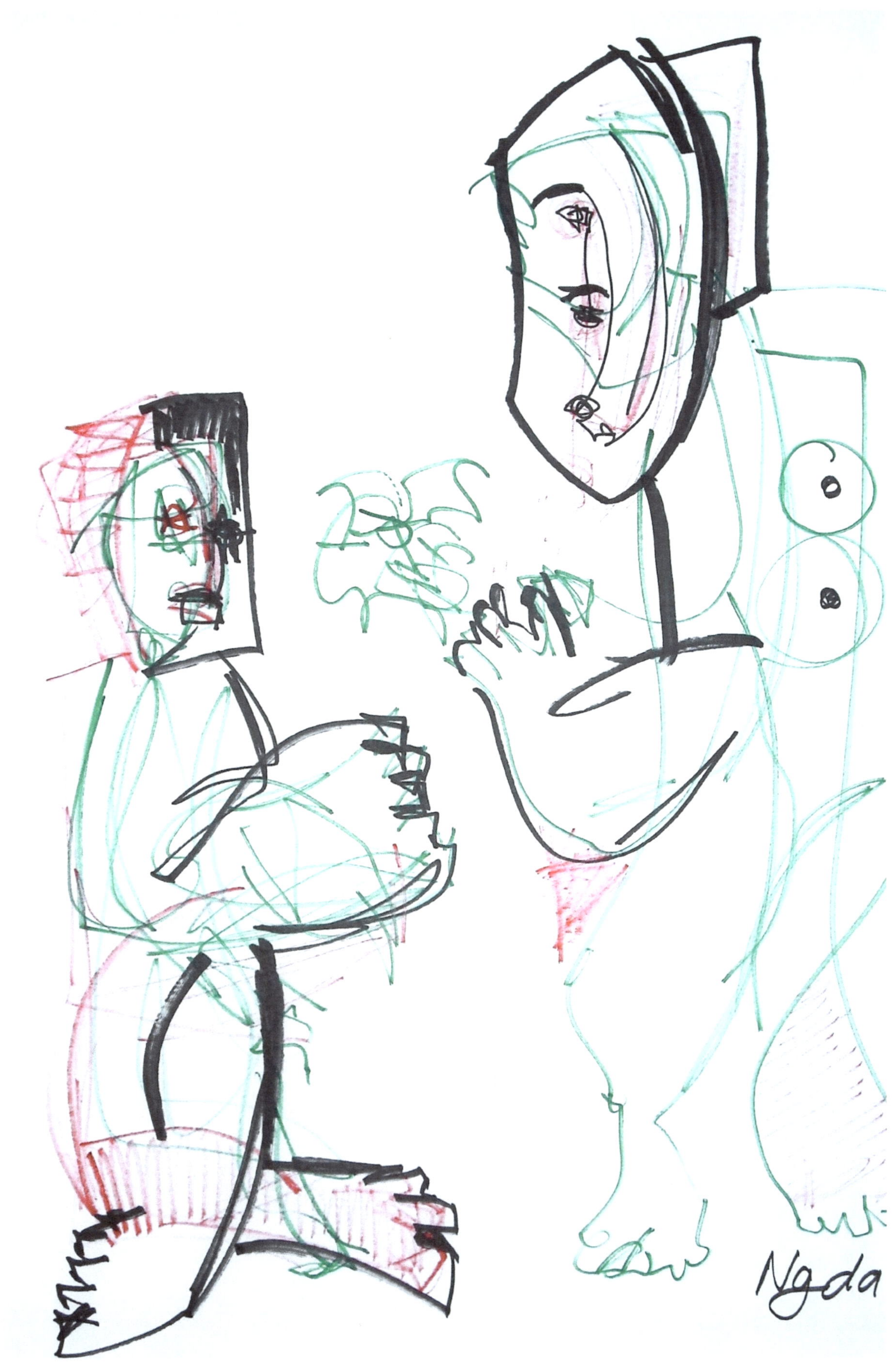

"THE DOVE ESCAPES"
Ngda

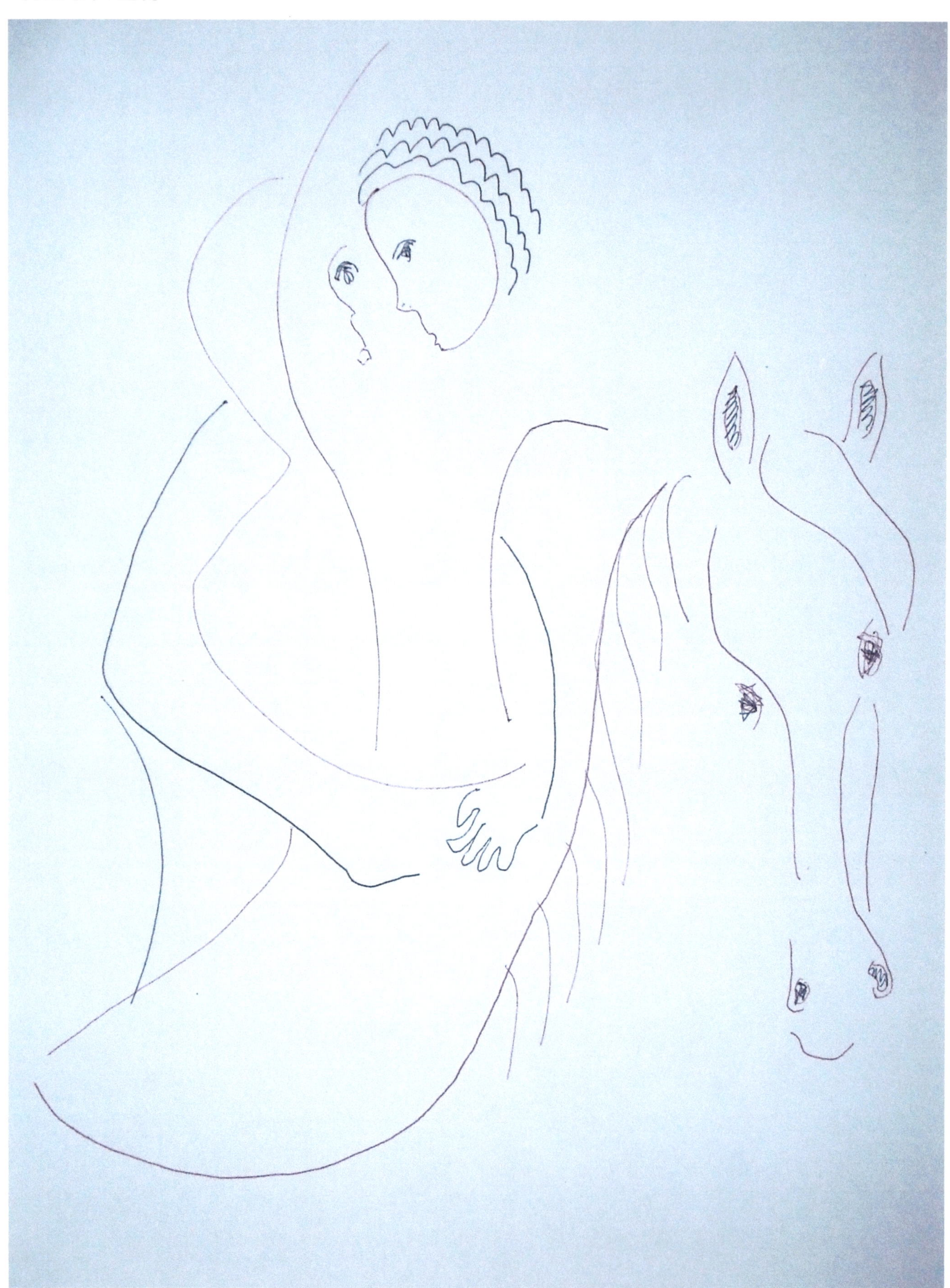

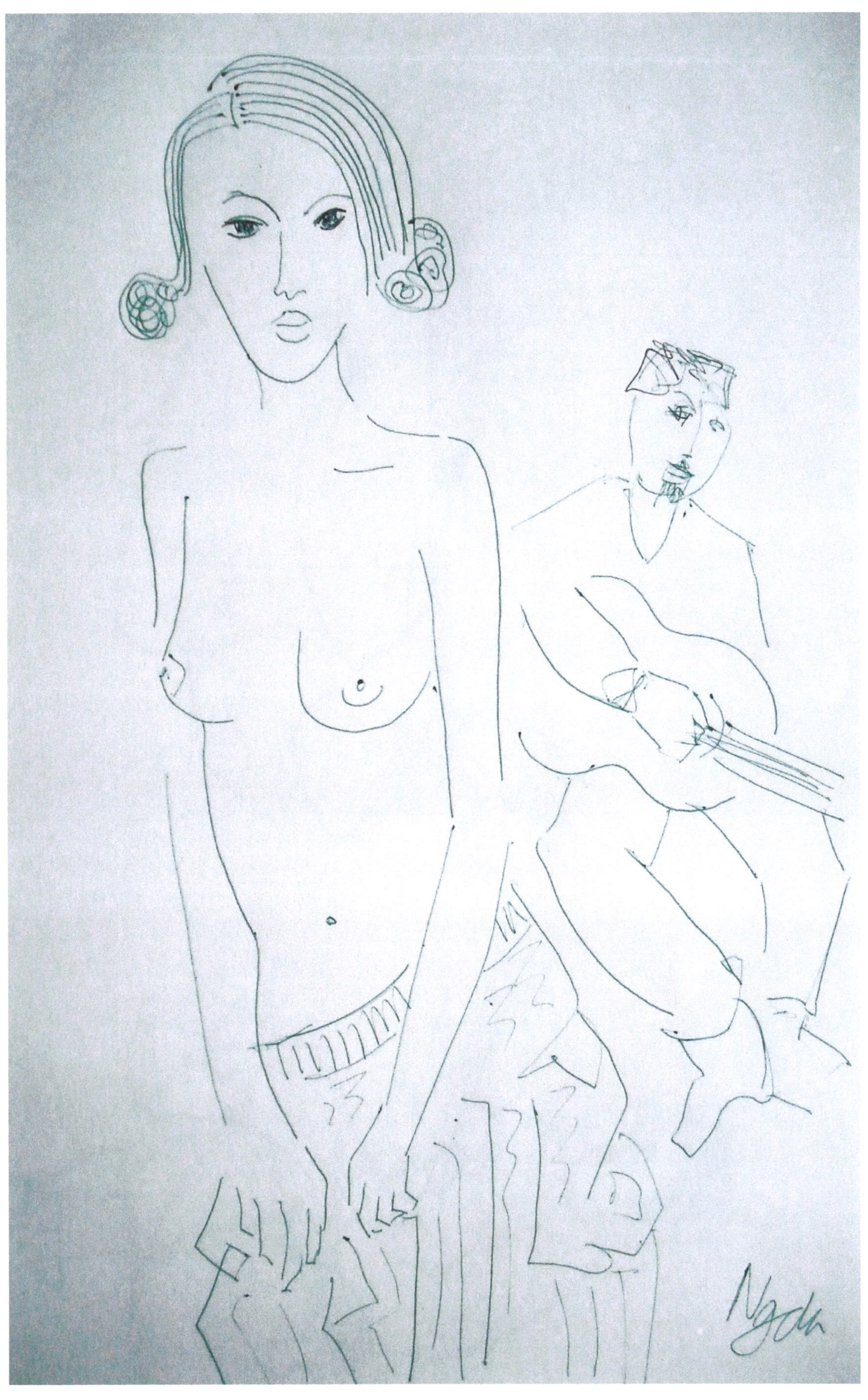

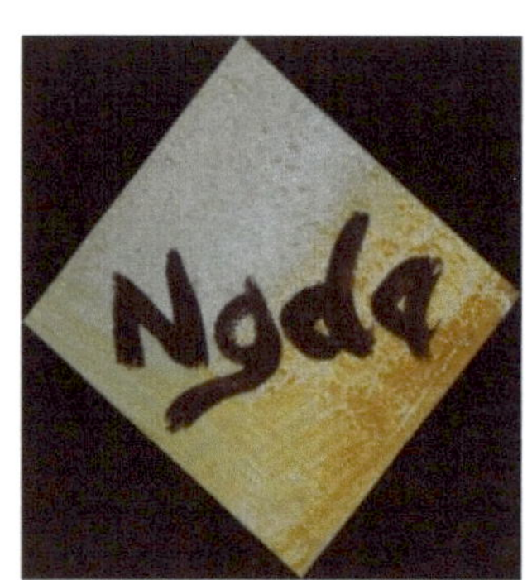

Najda in Line

"At the Circus"

Agora Gallery

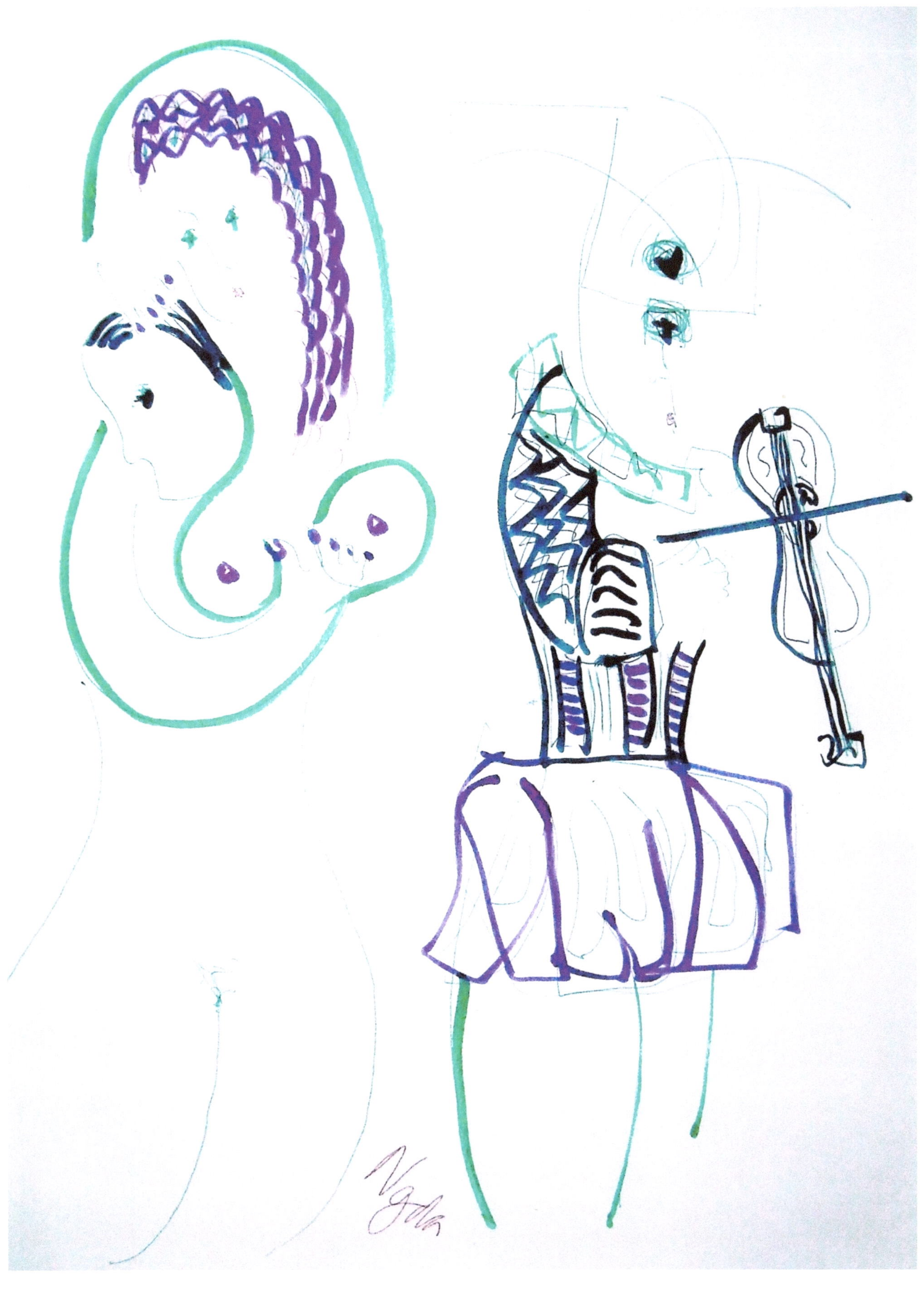

"THE ACROBAT"

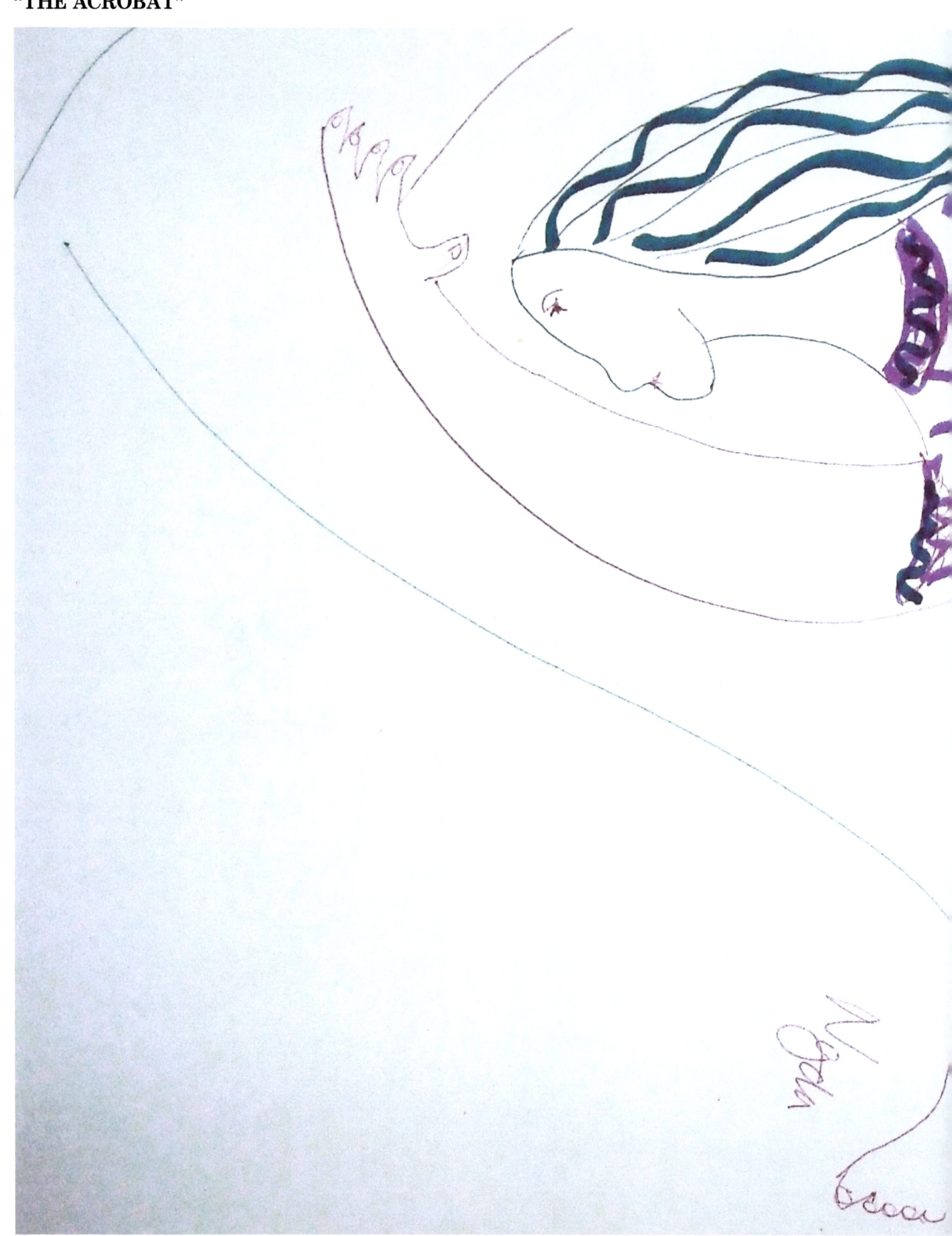

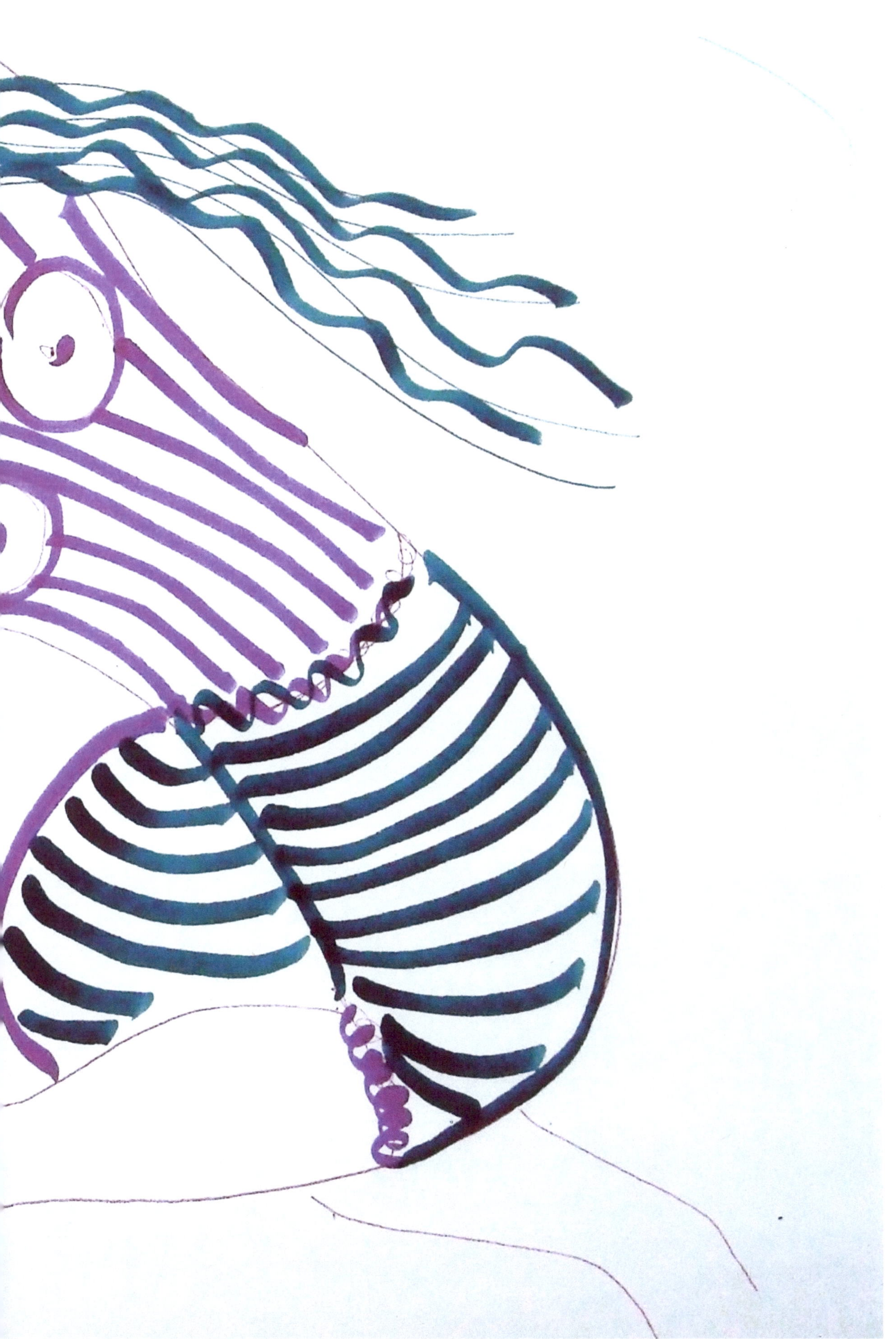

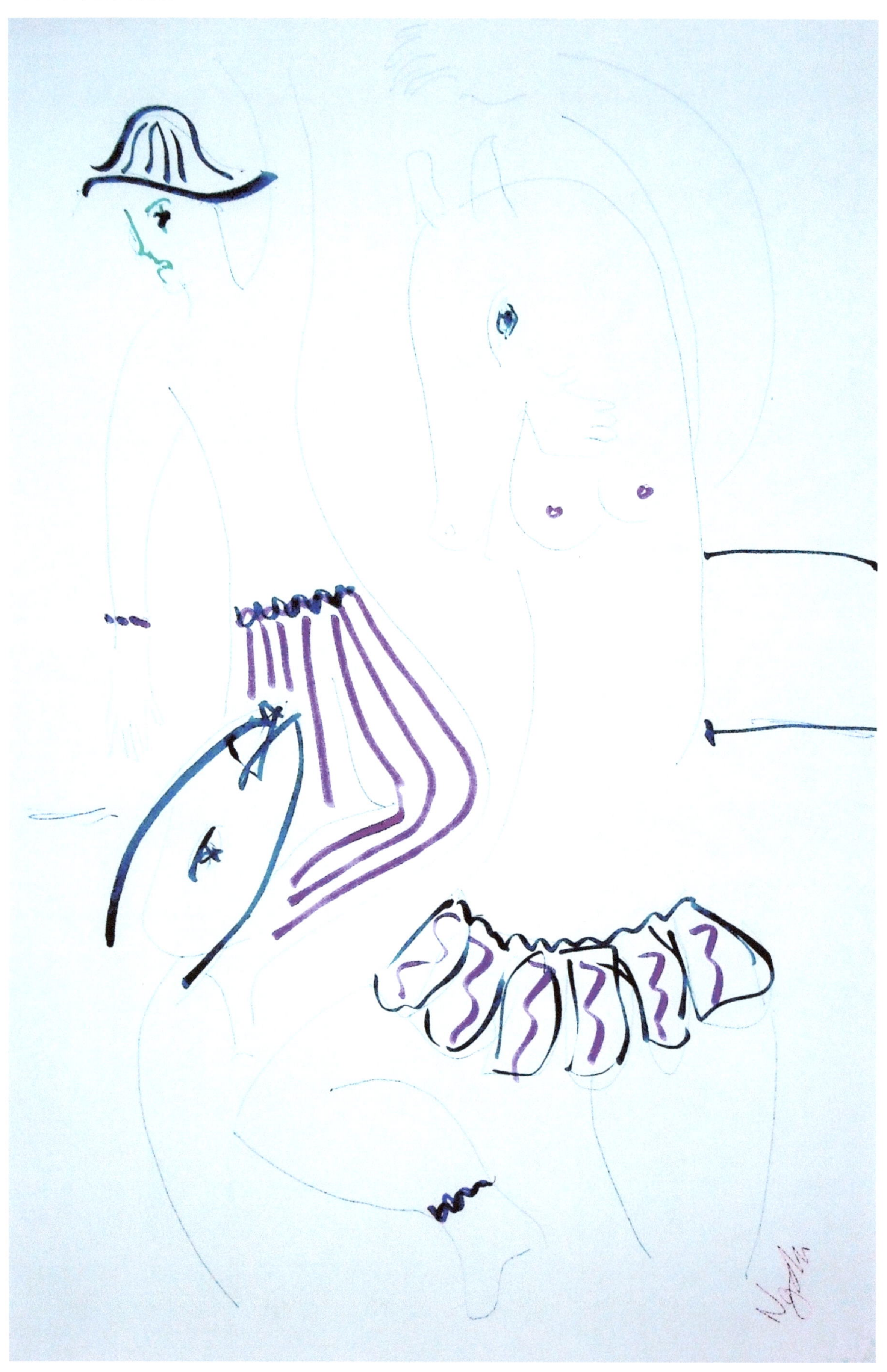

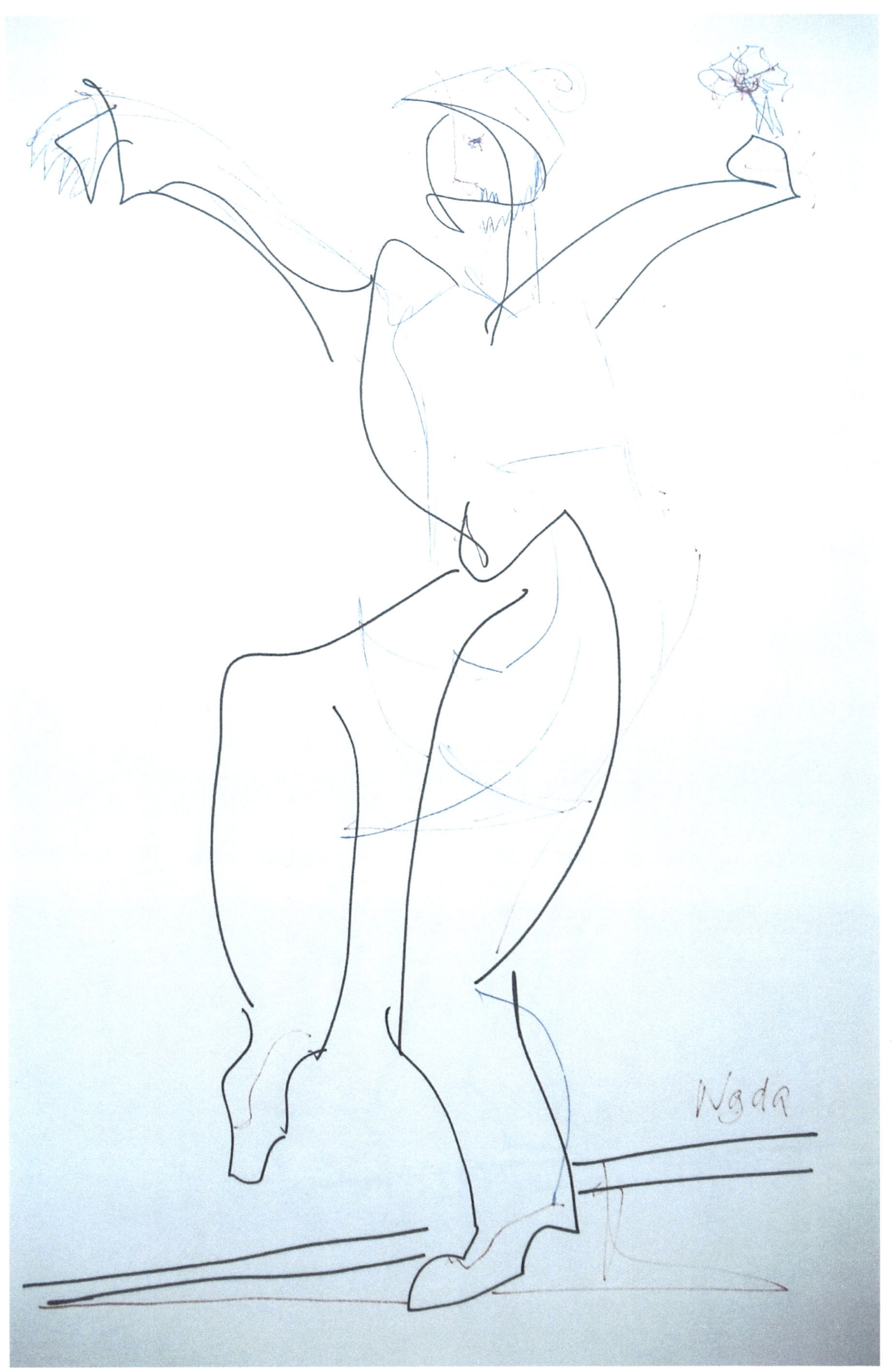

"CLOWN ON THE GROUND"

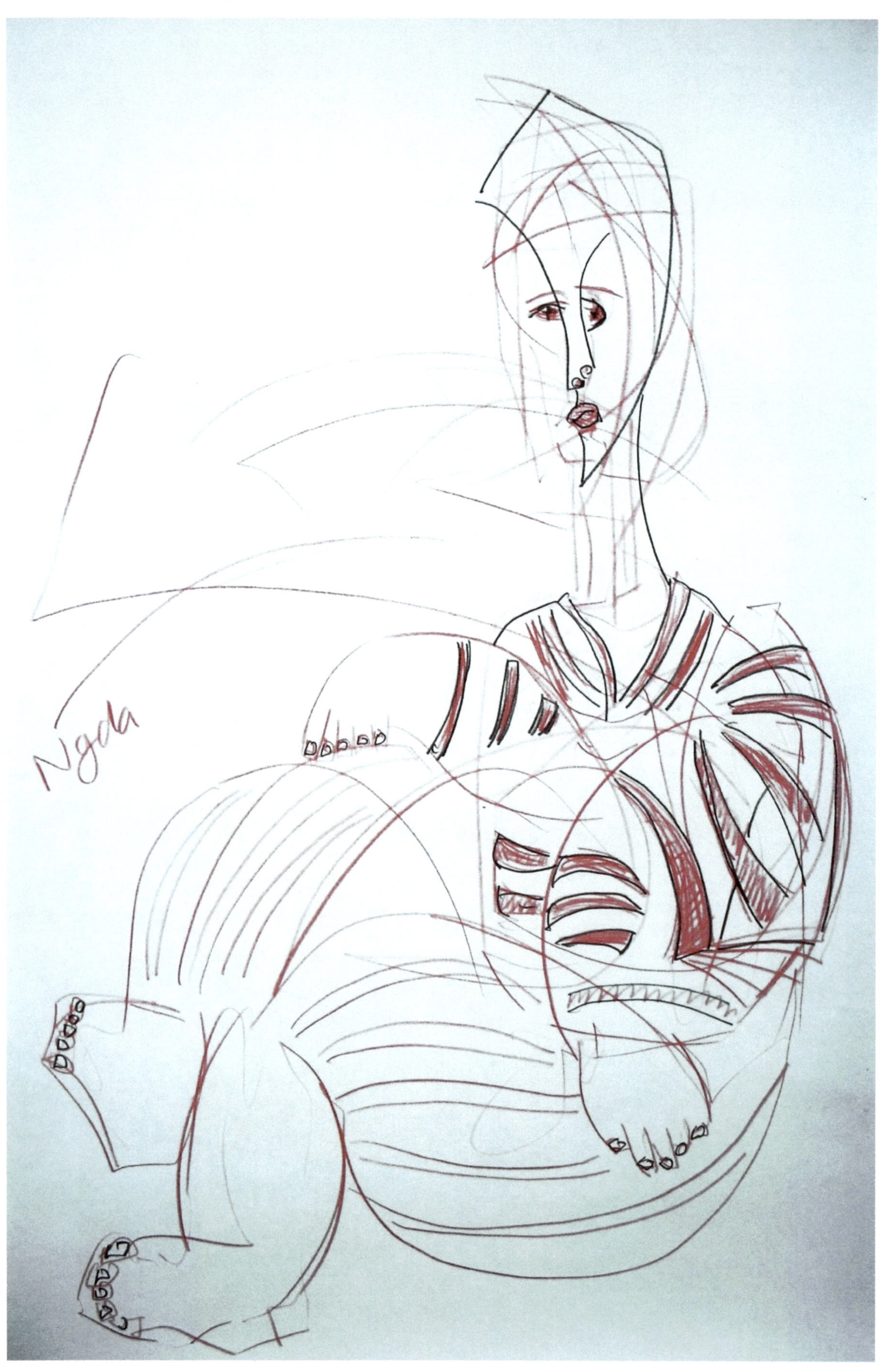

Najda in Line

"La figlia che piange"

(The weeping daughter)

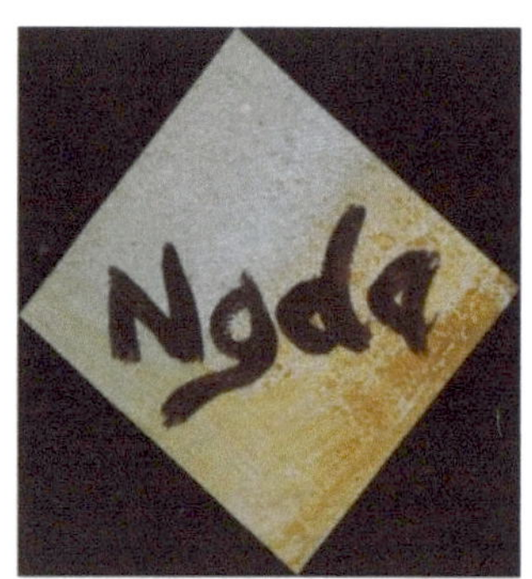
Node

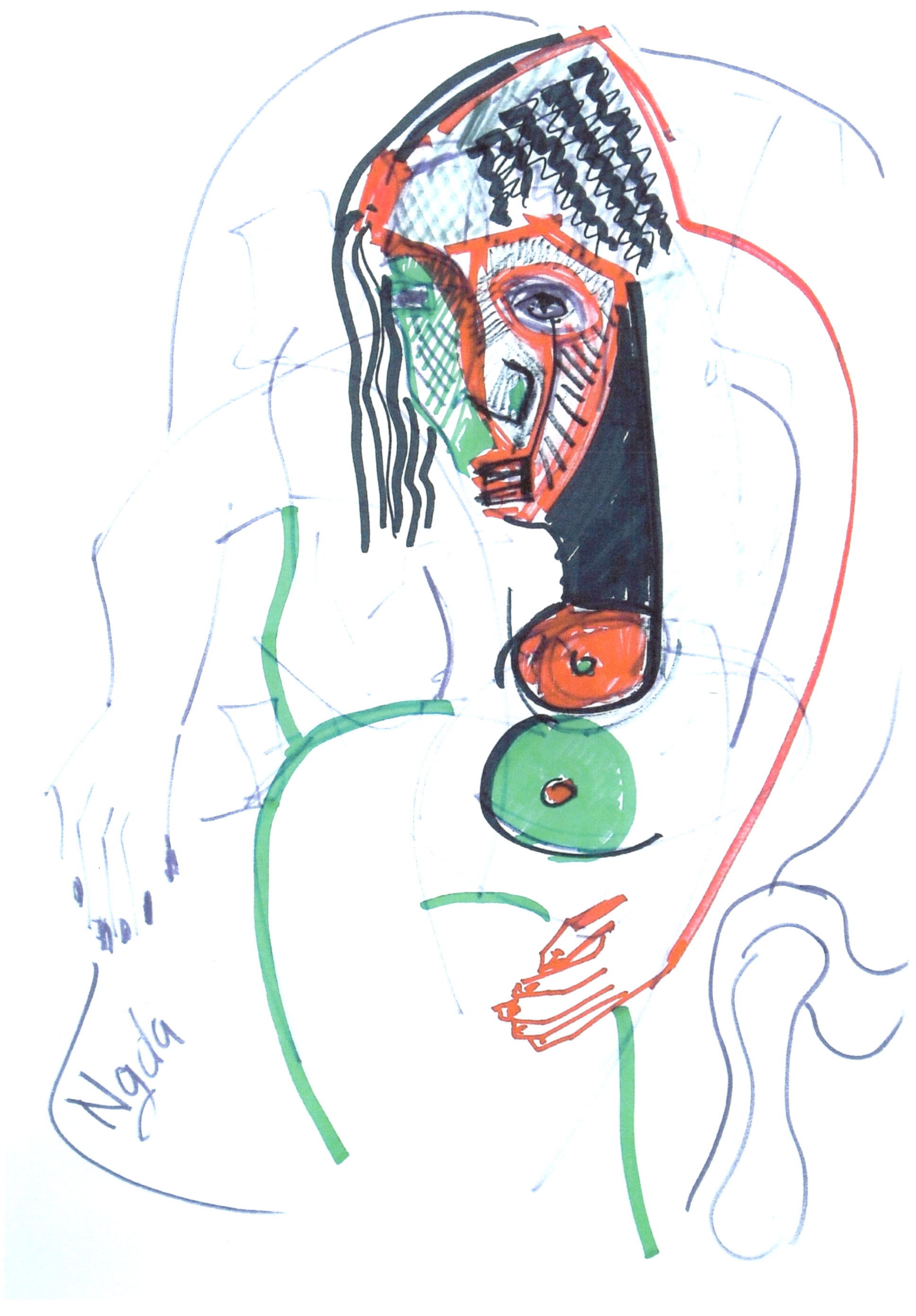

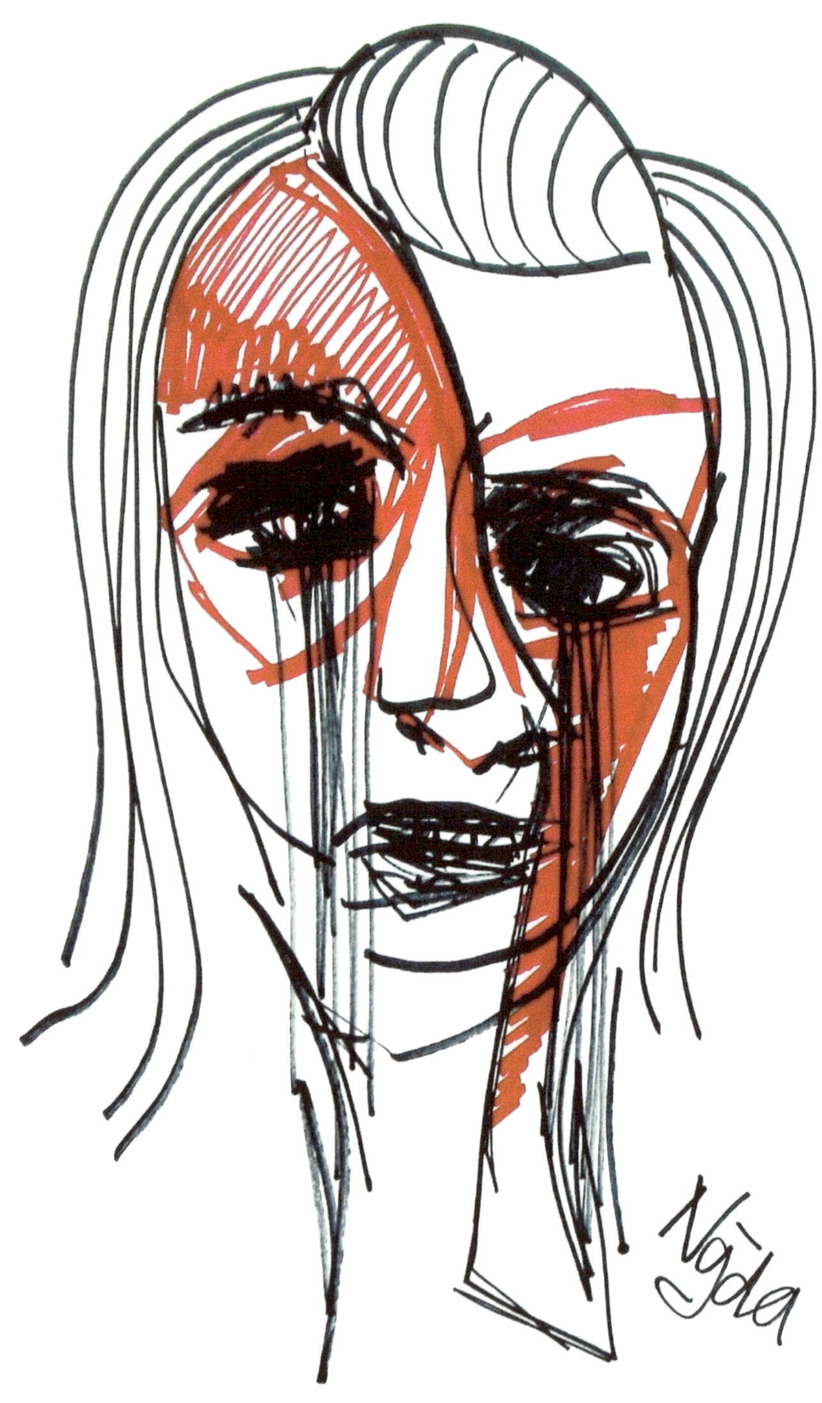

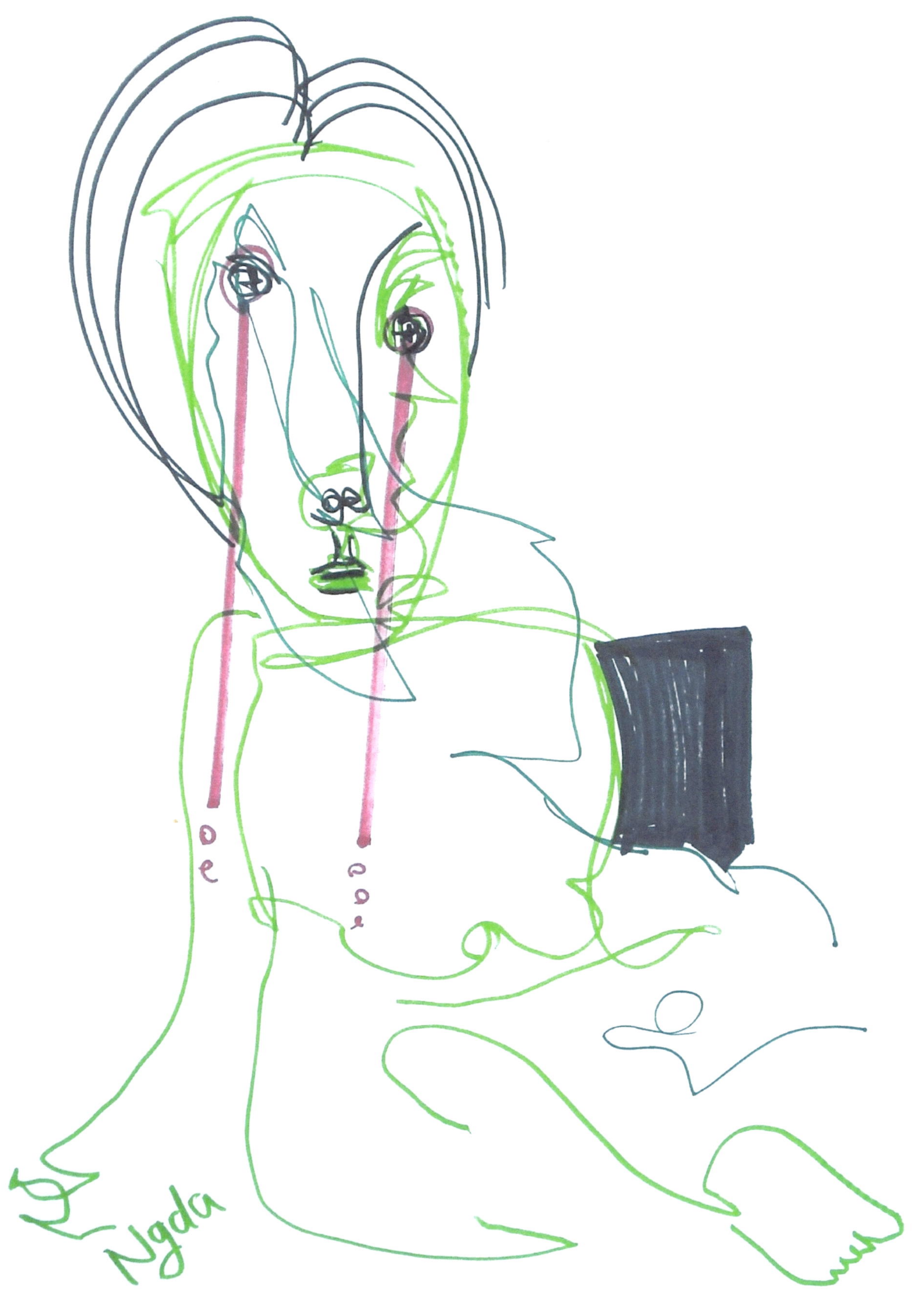

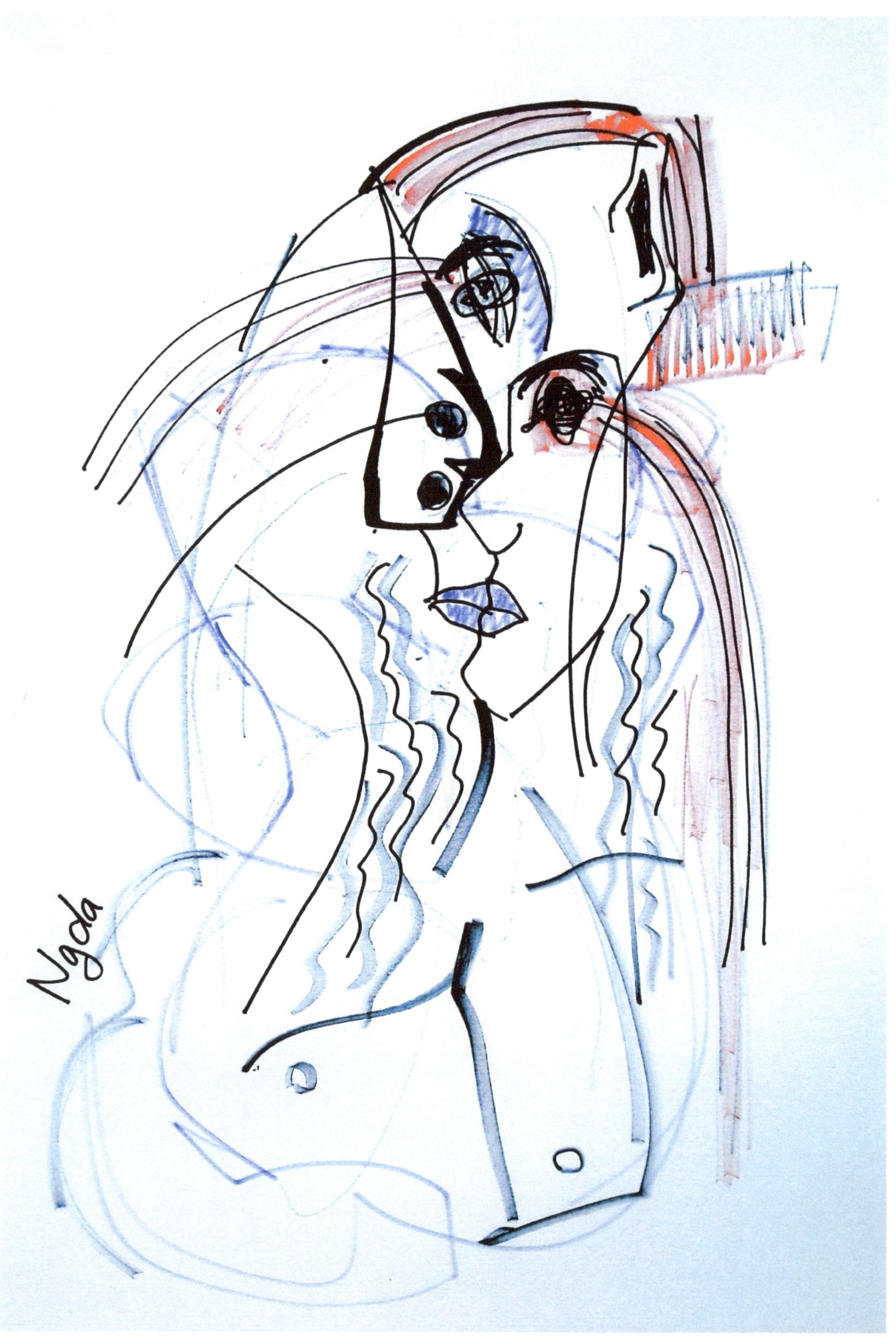

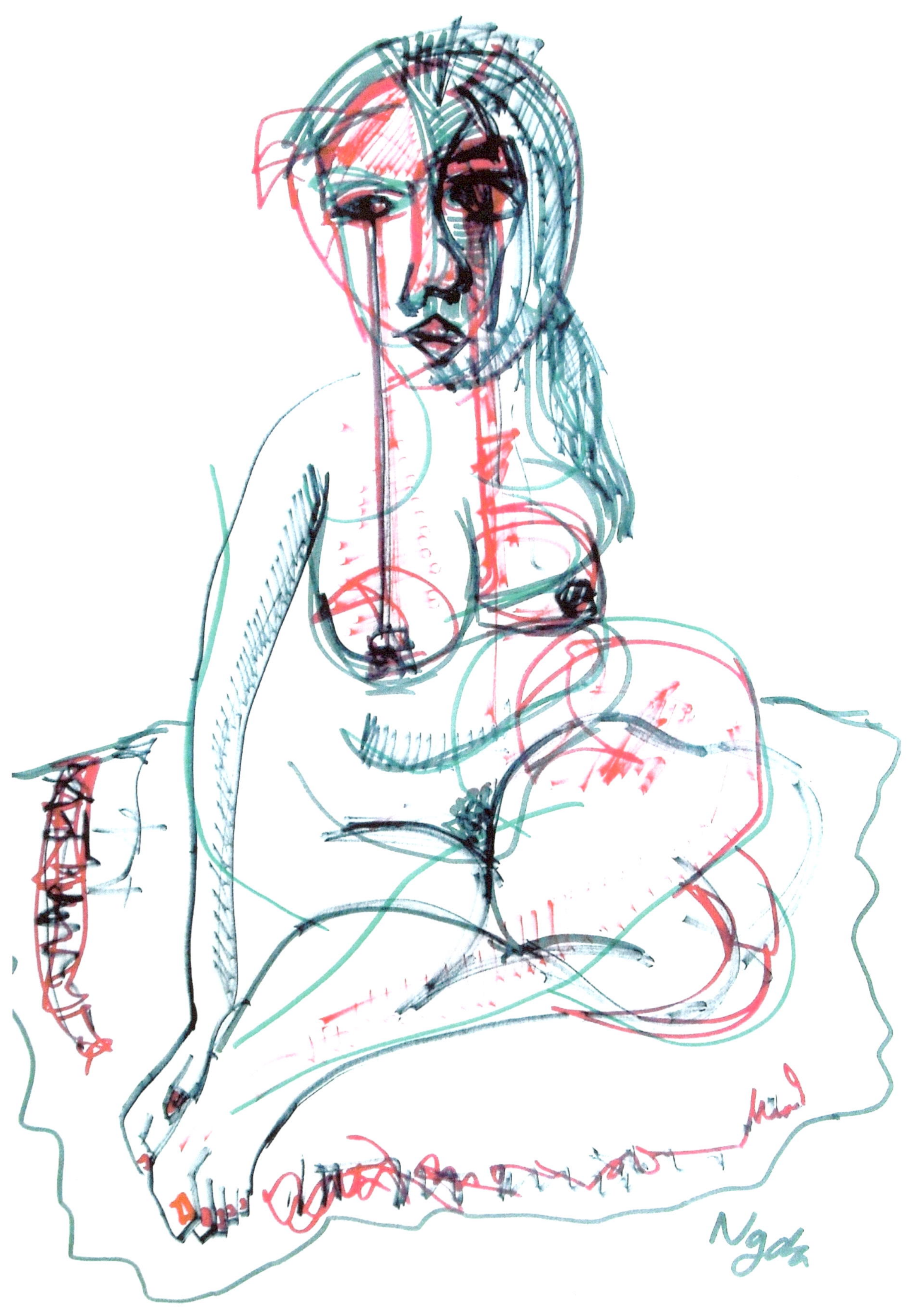

Agora Gallery

Najda in Line

"Spirited Bodies"

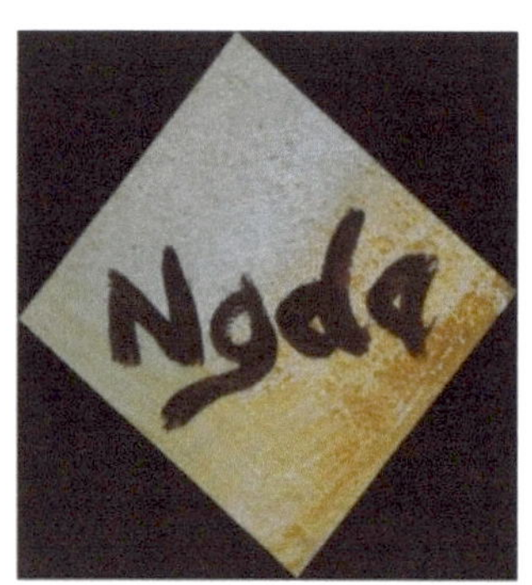

Ngda

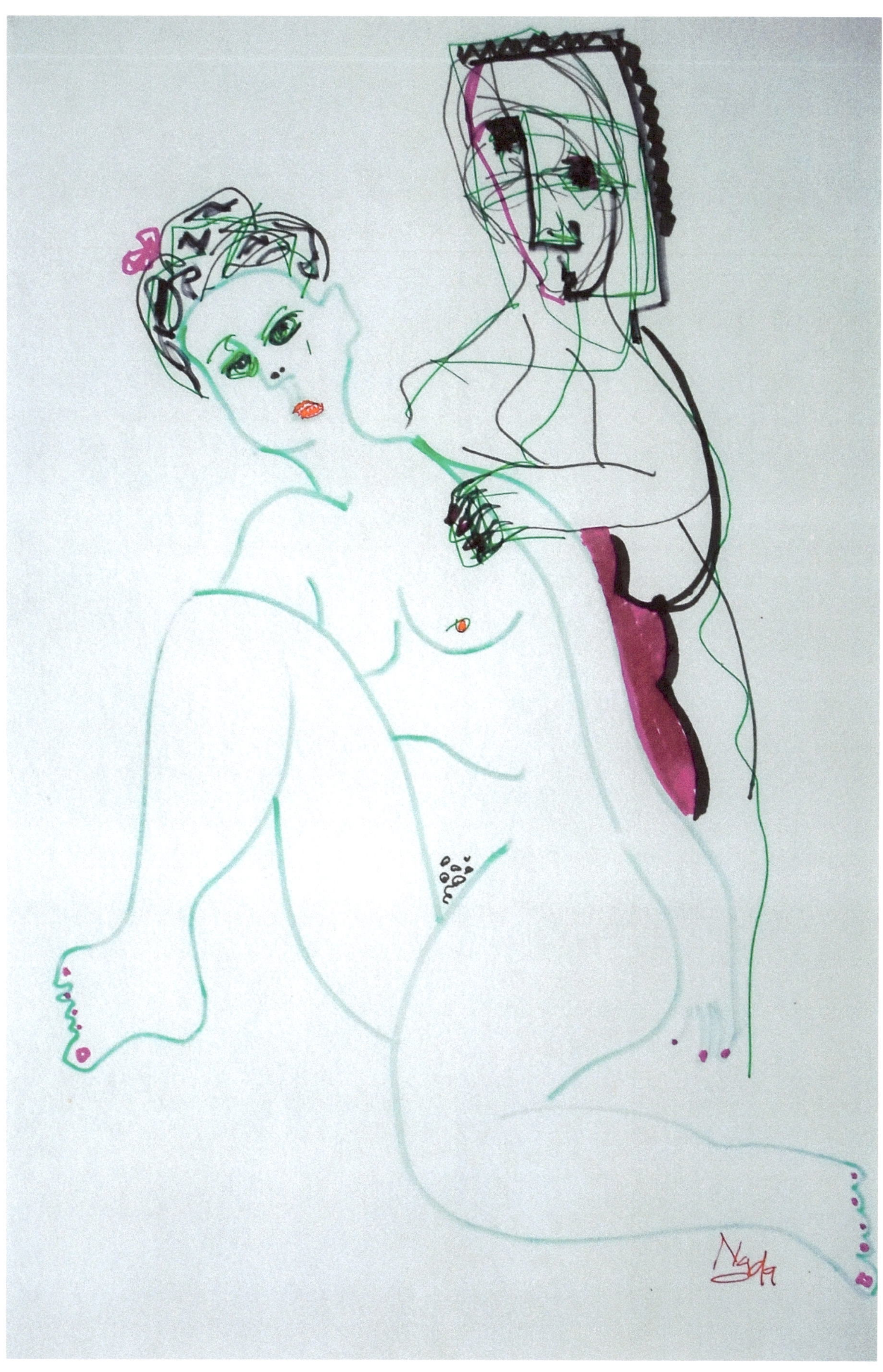

"THE COSMIC GARDEN"

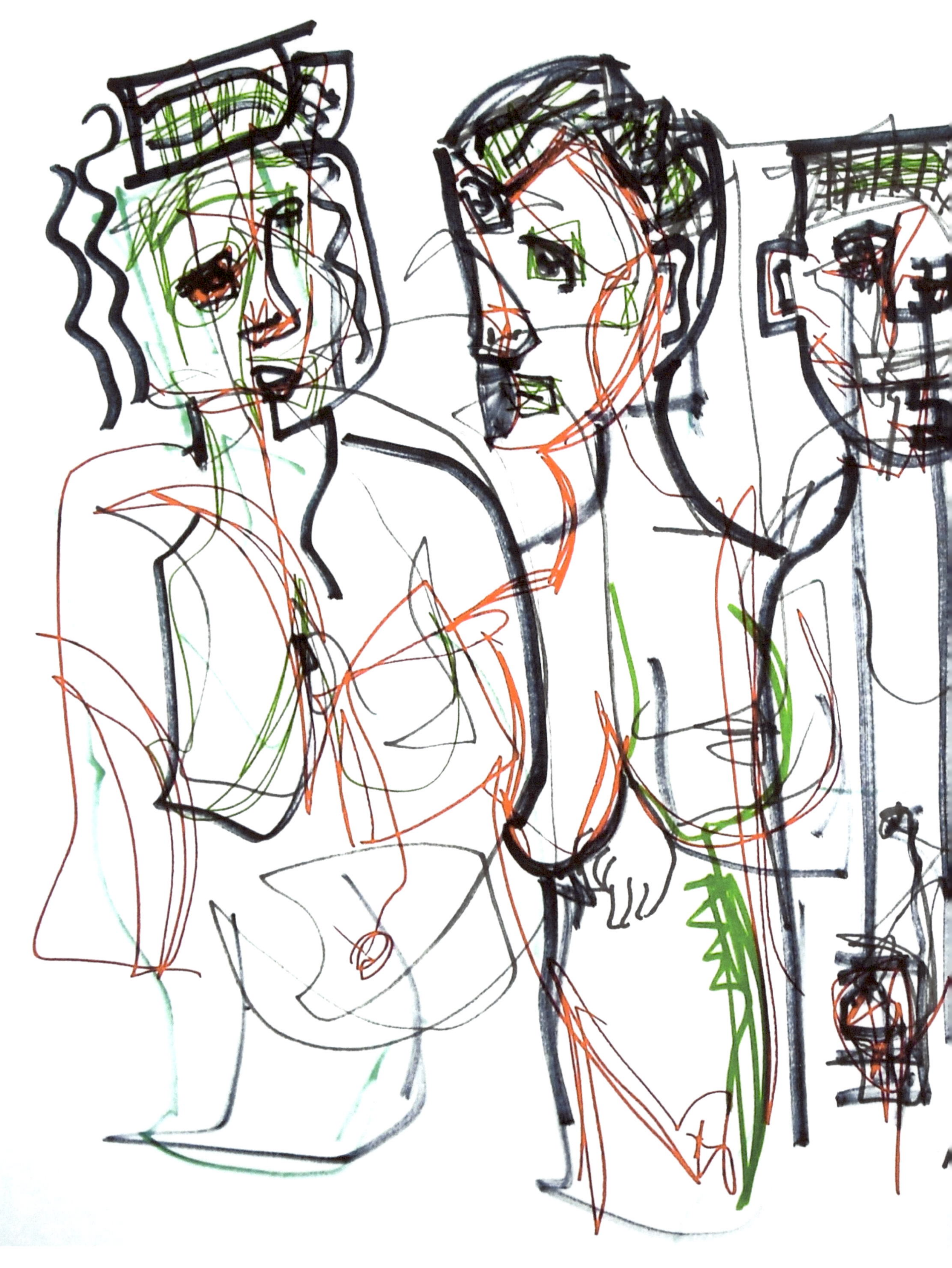

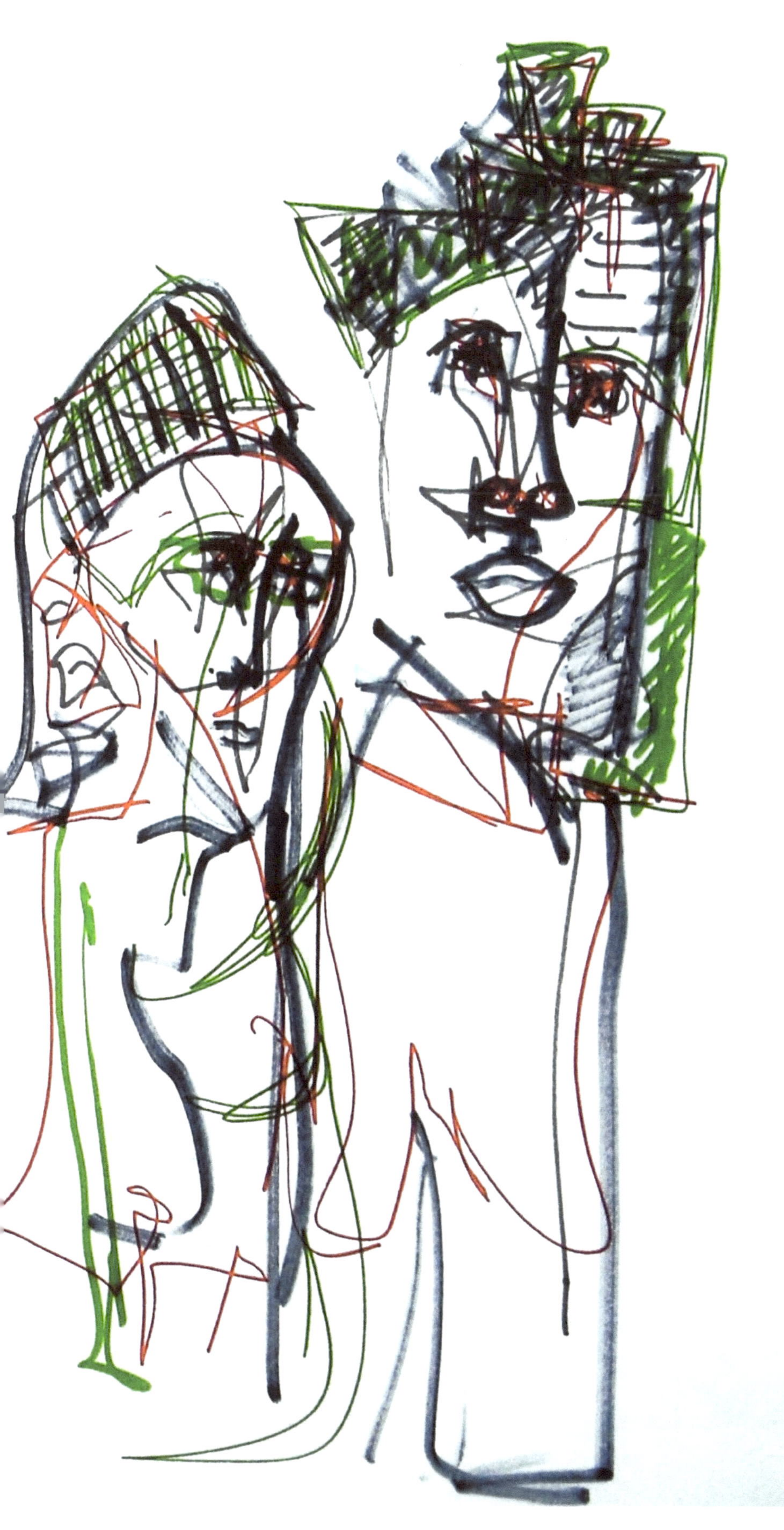

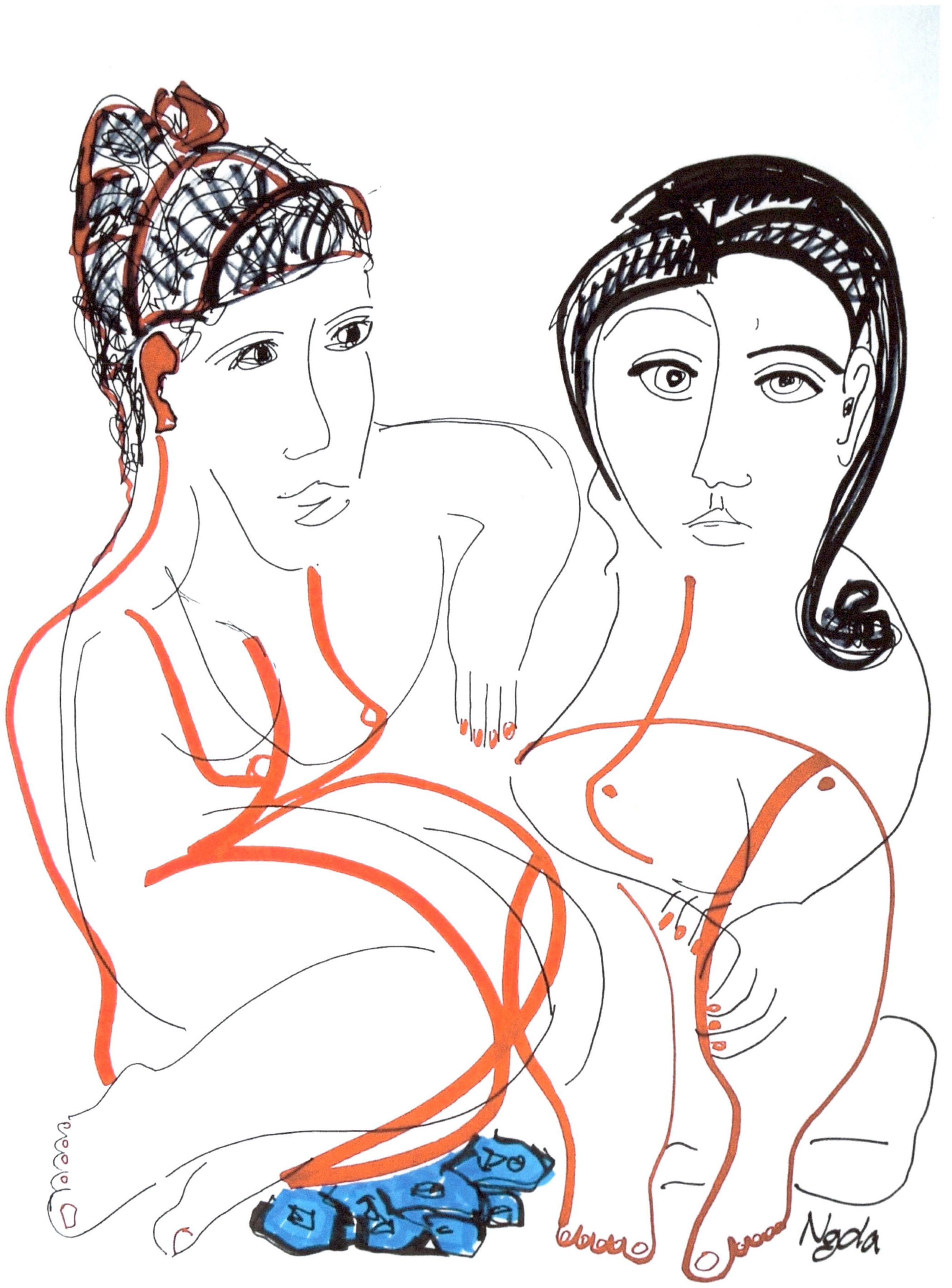

Ngola

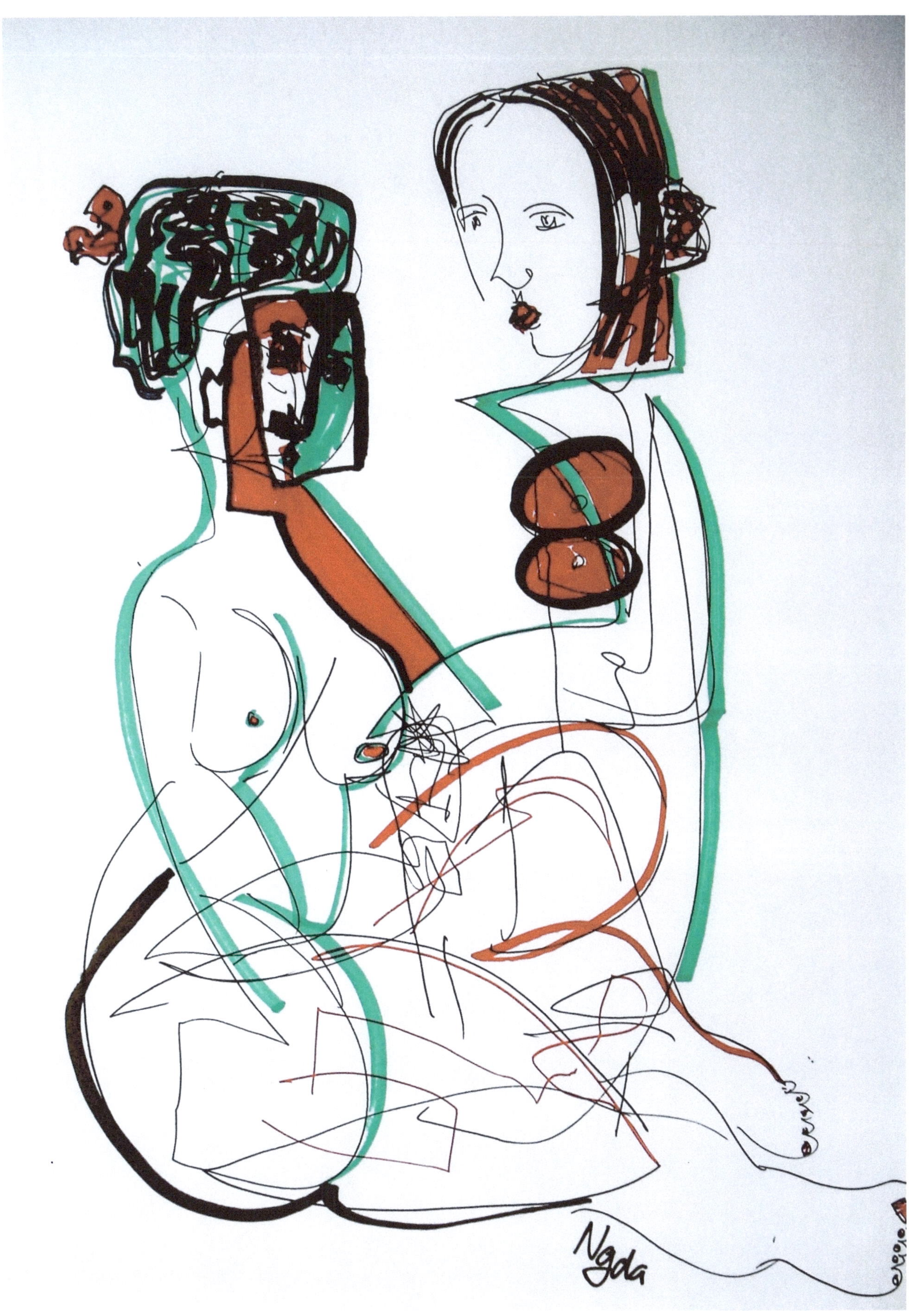

"TOMORROW THE SUN WILL RISE"

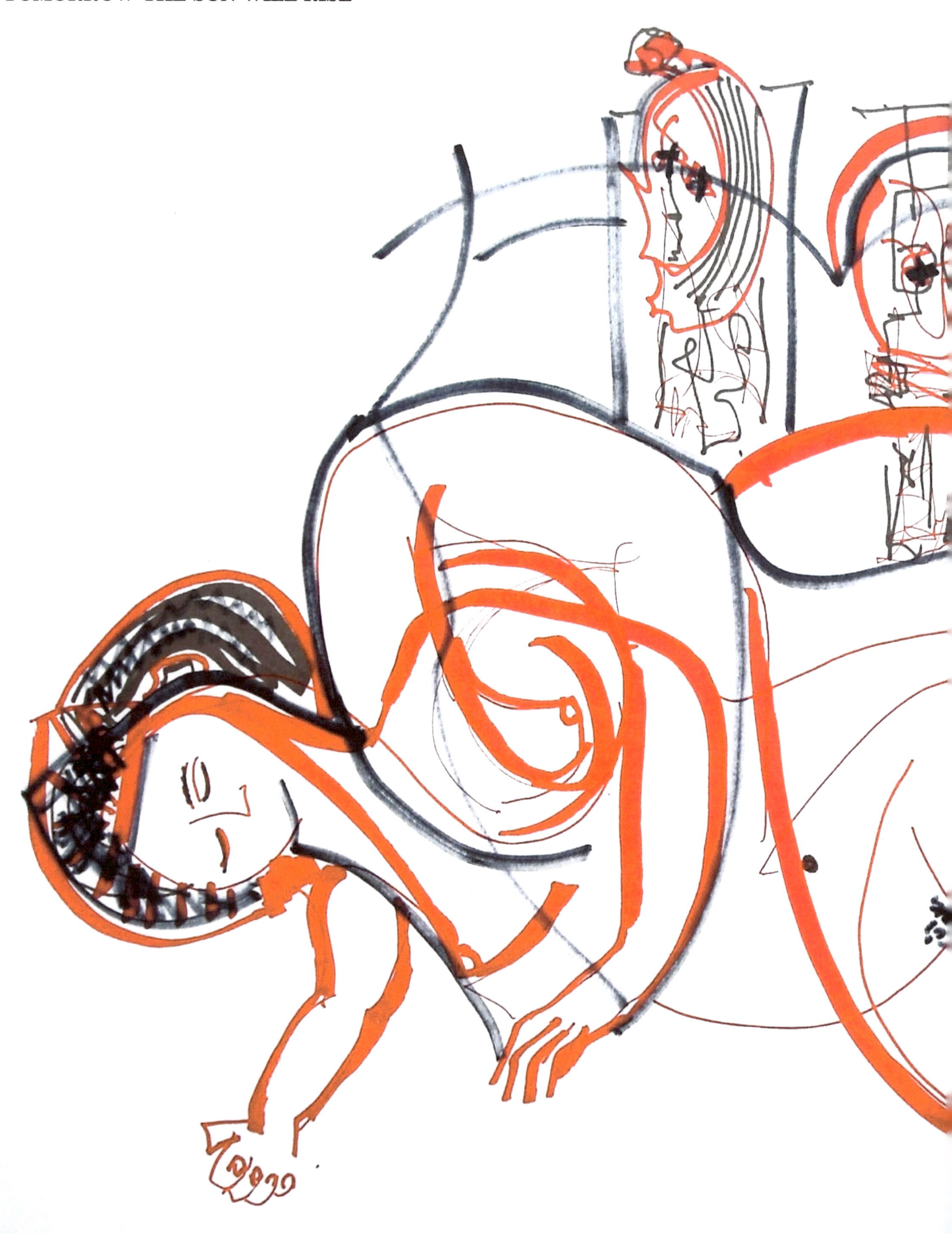

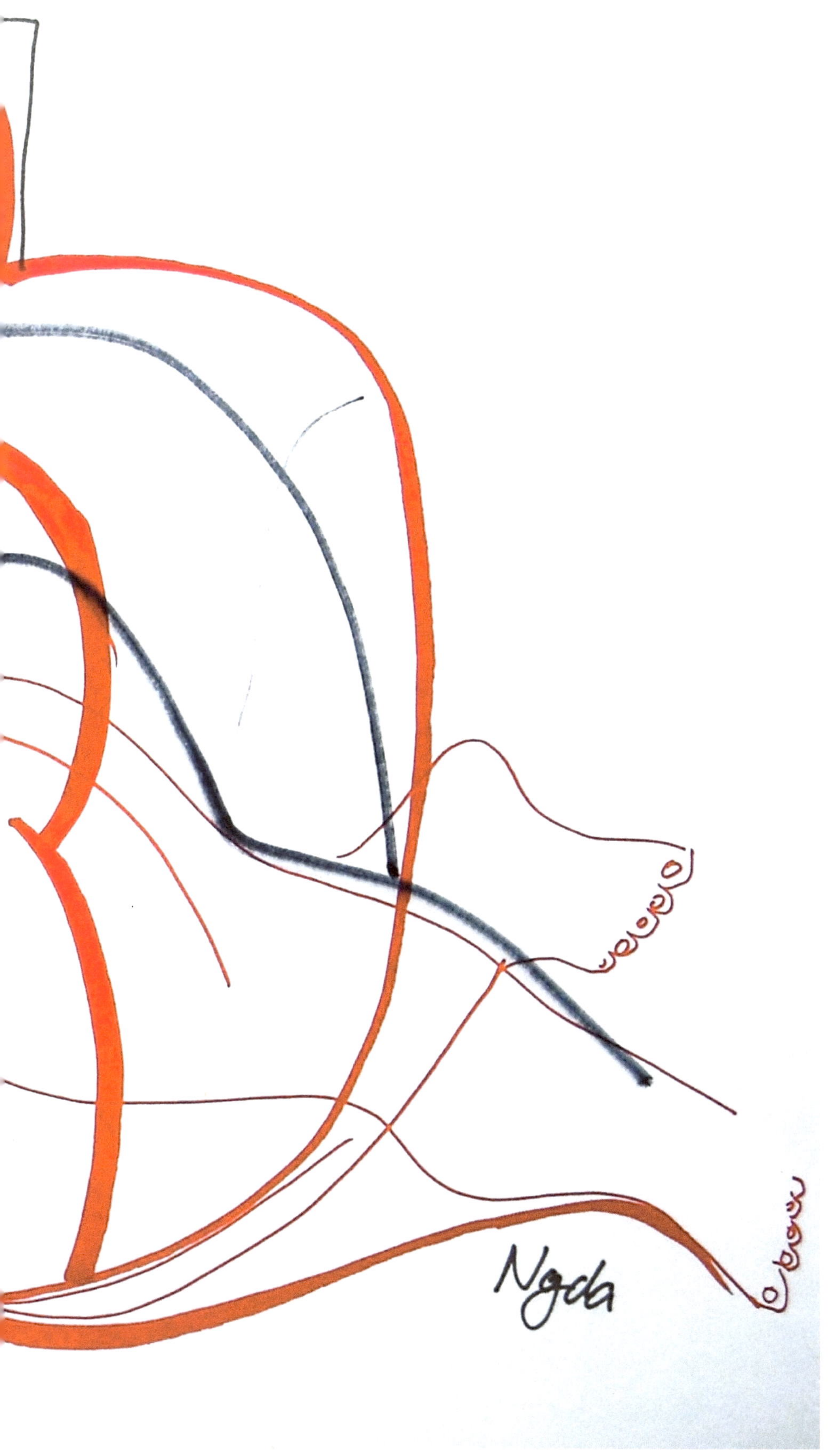

Ngda

“THE FIELDS OF SPRING”

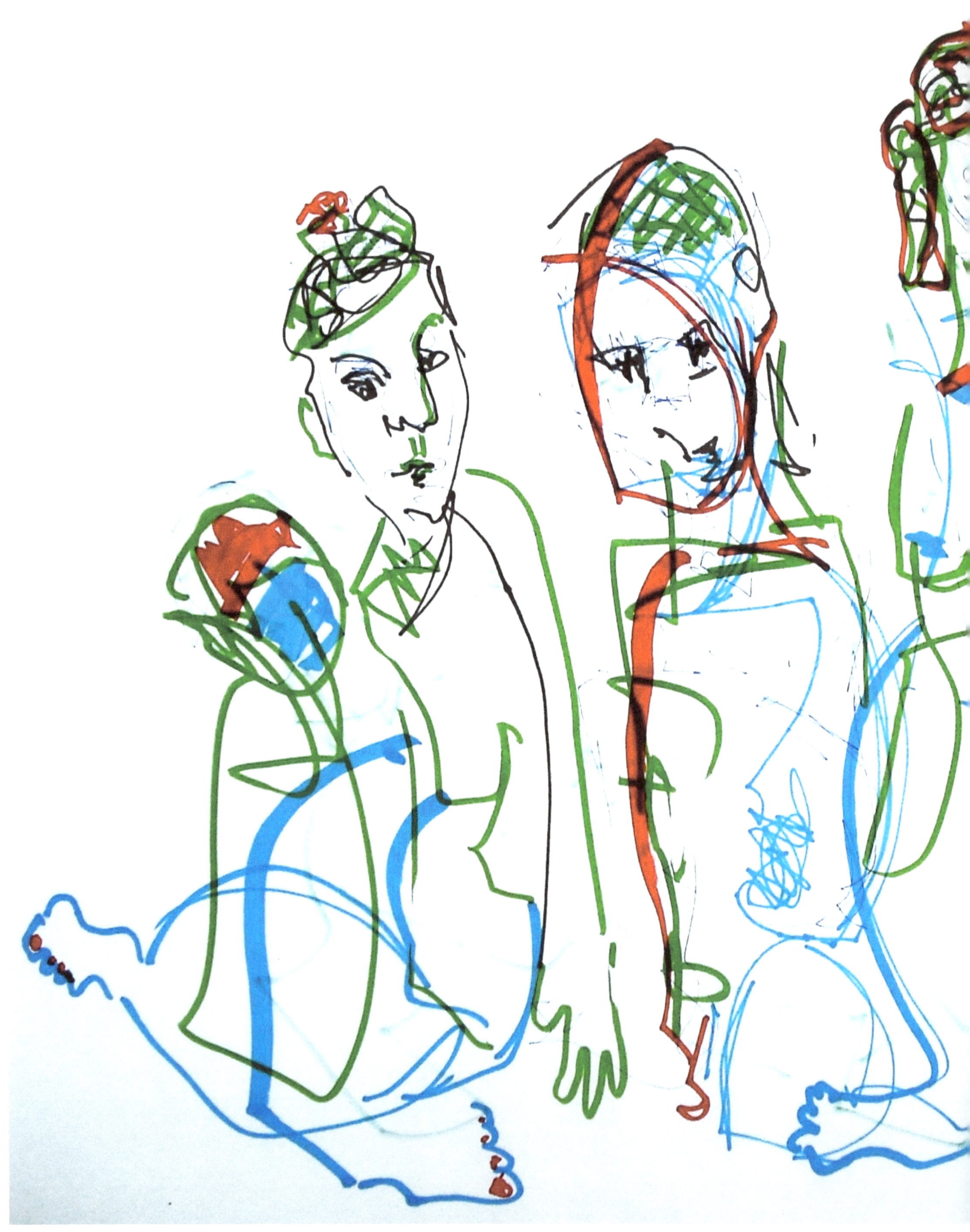

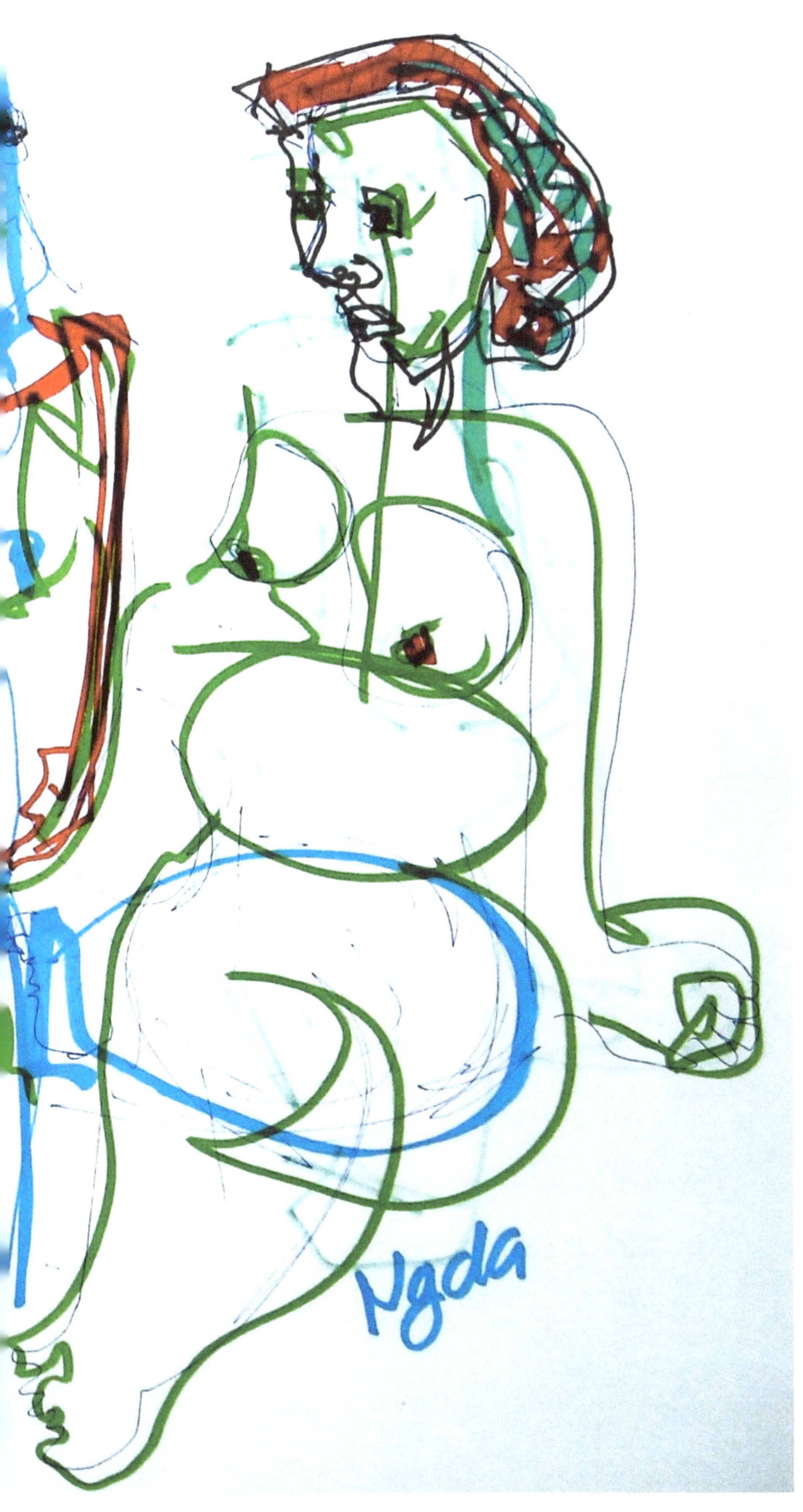
Ngda

"MISTRESS OF BLUE"

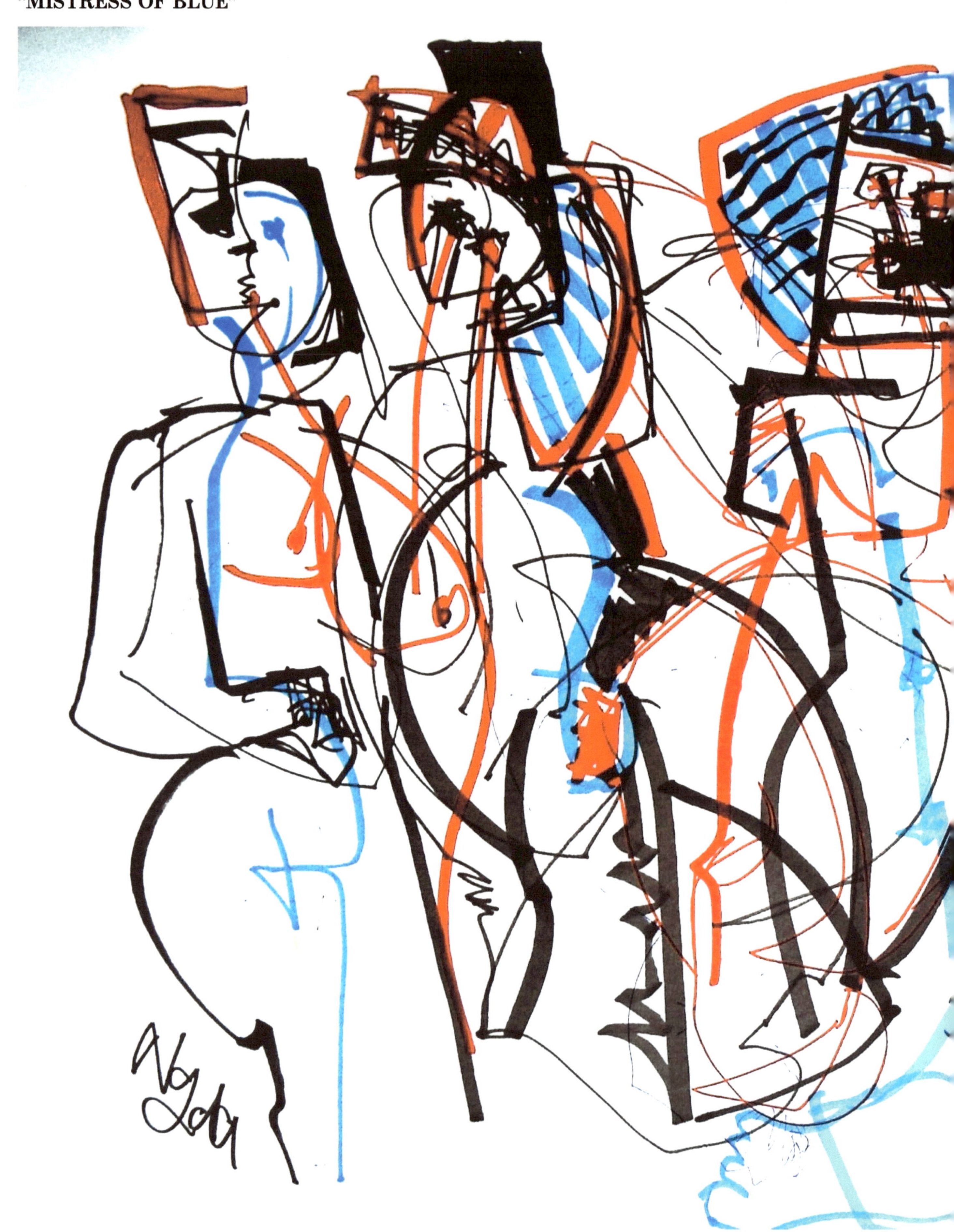

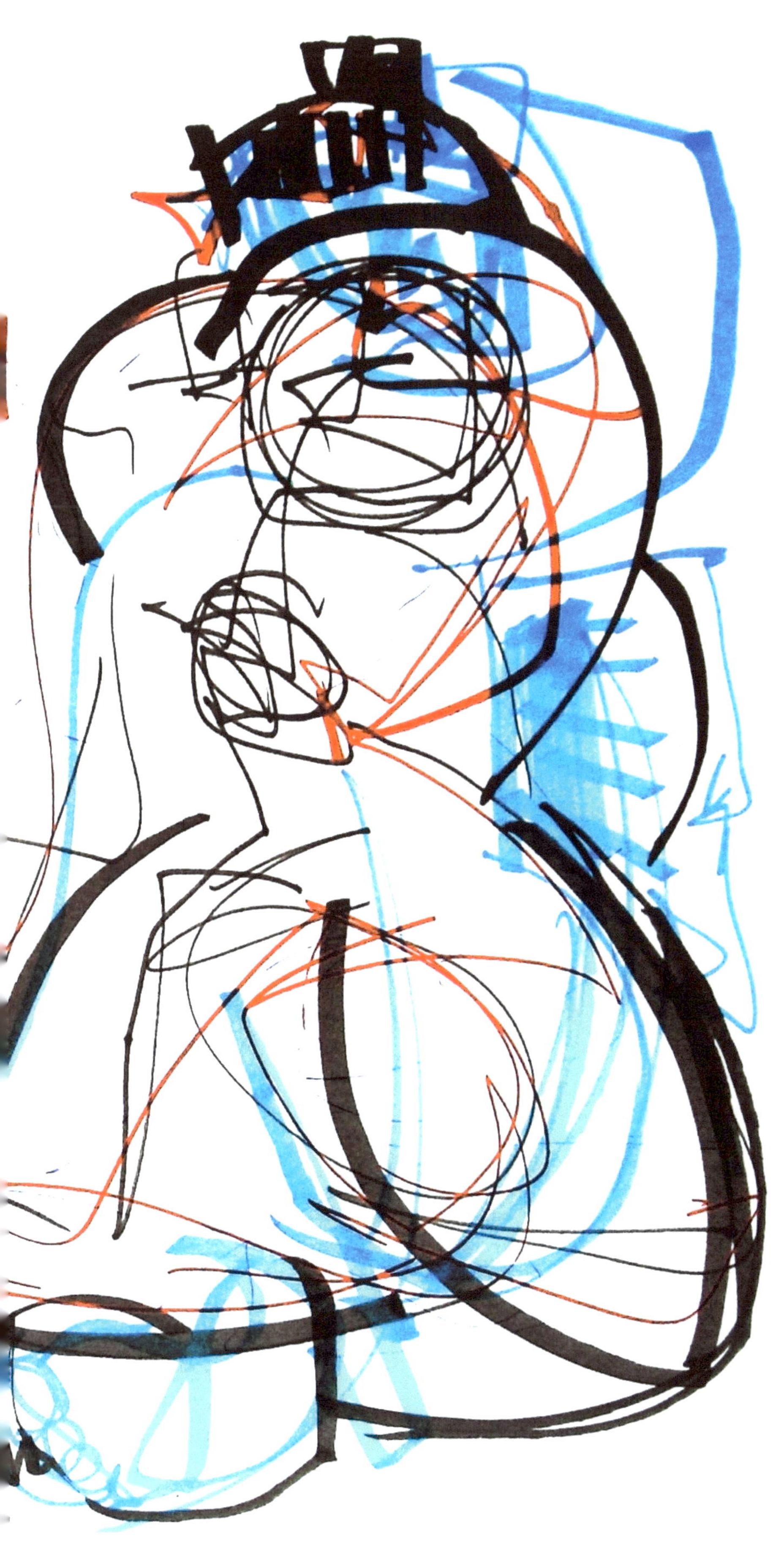

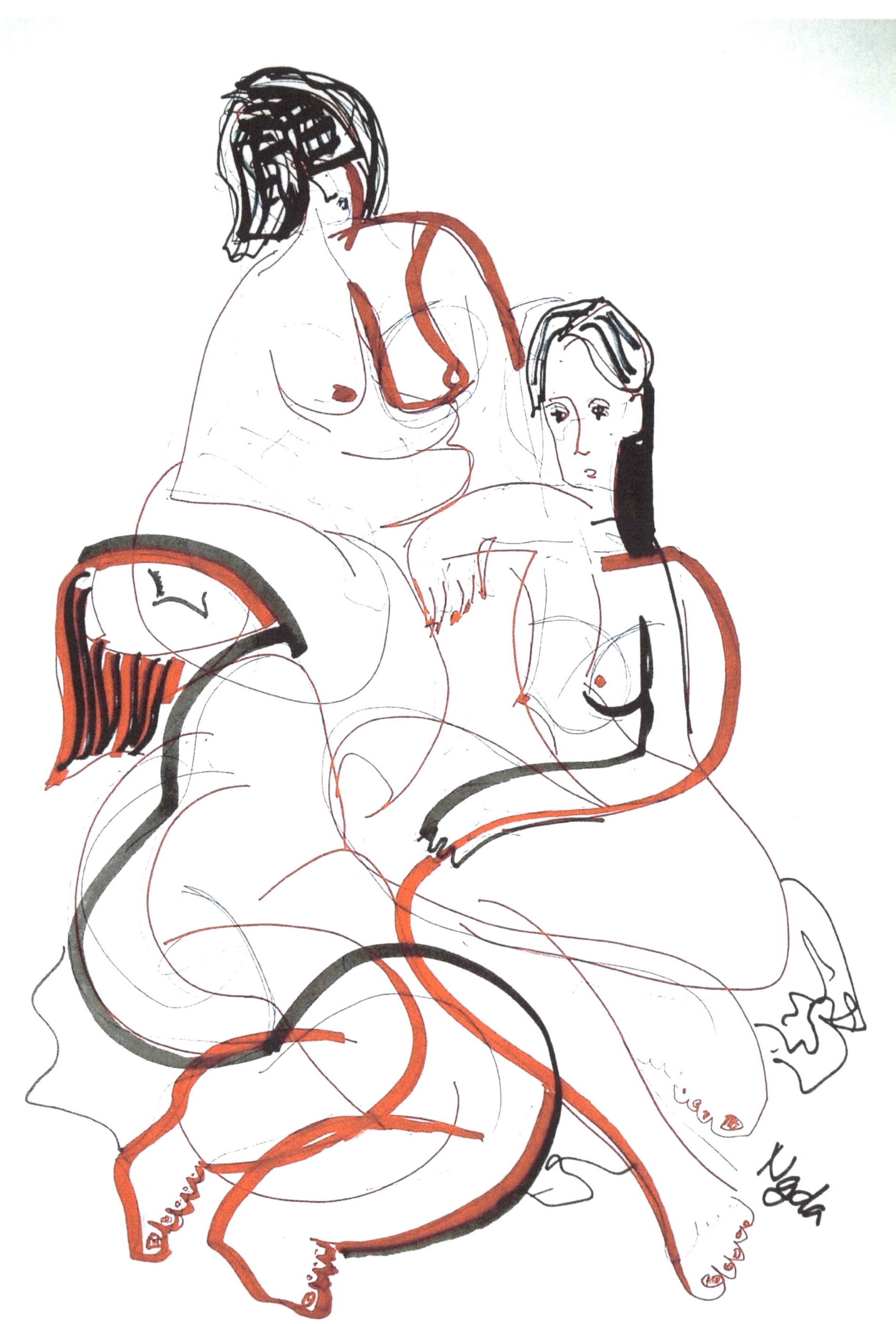

Najda in Line

"Drama at the Pianodrome"

Agora Gallery

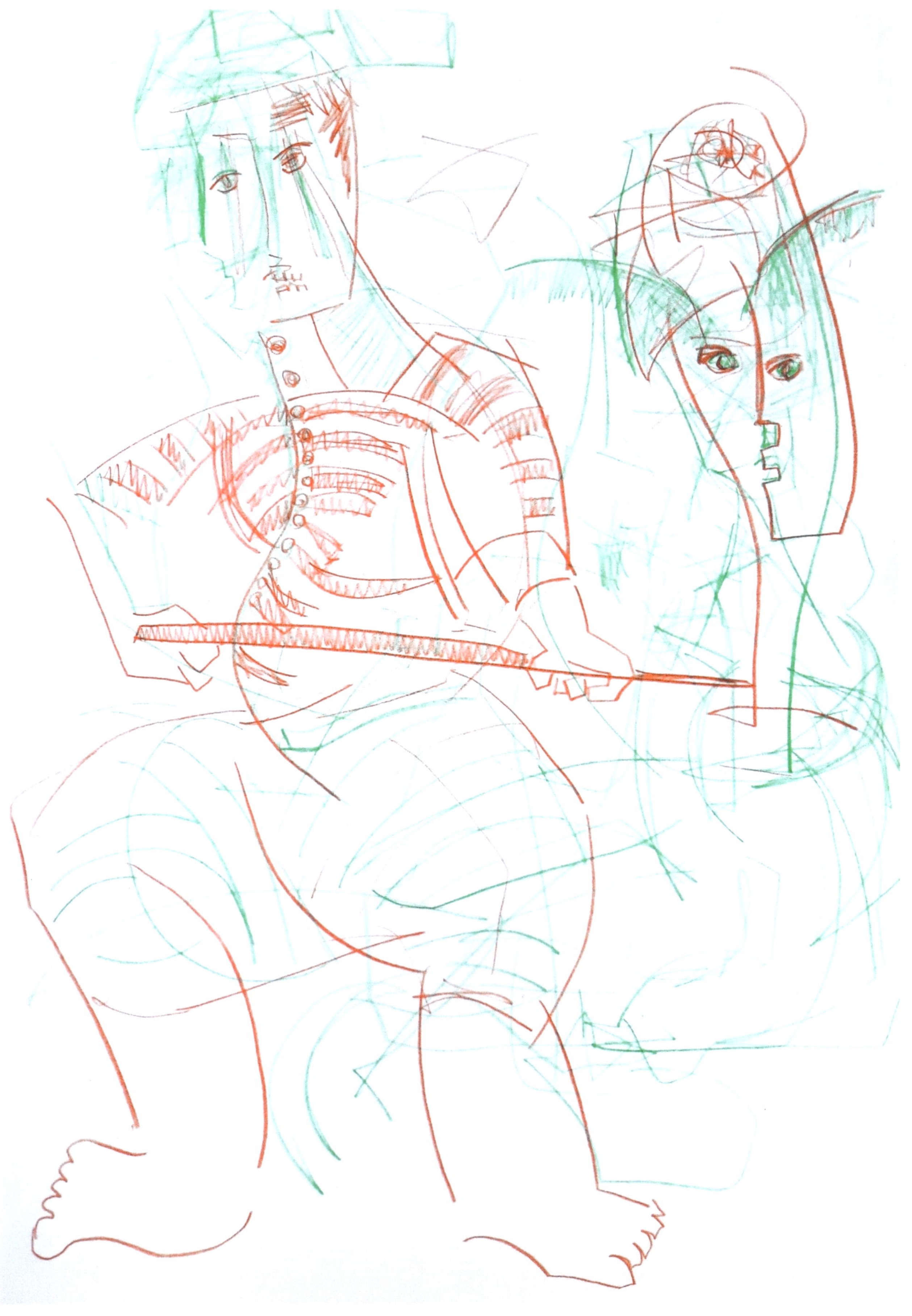

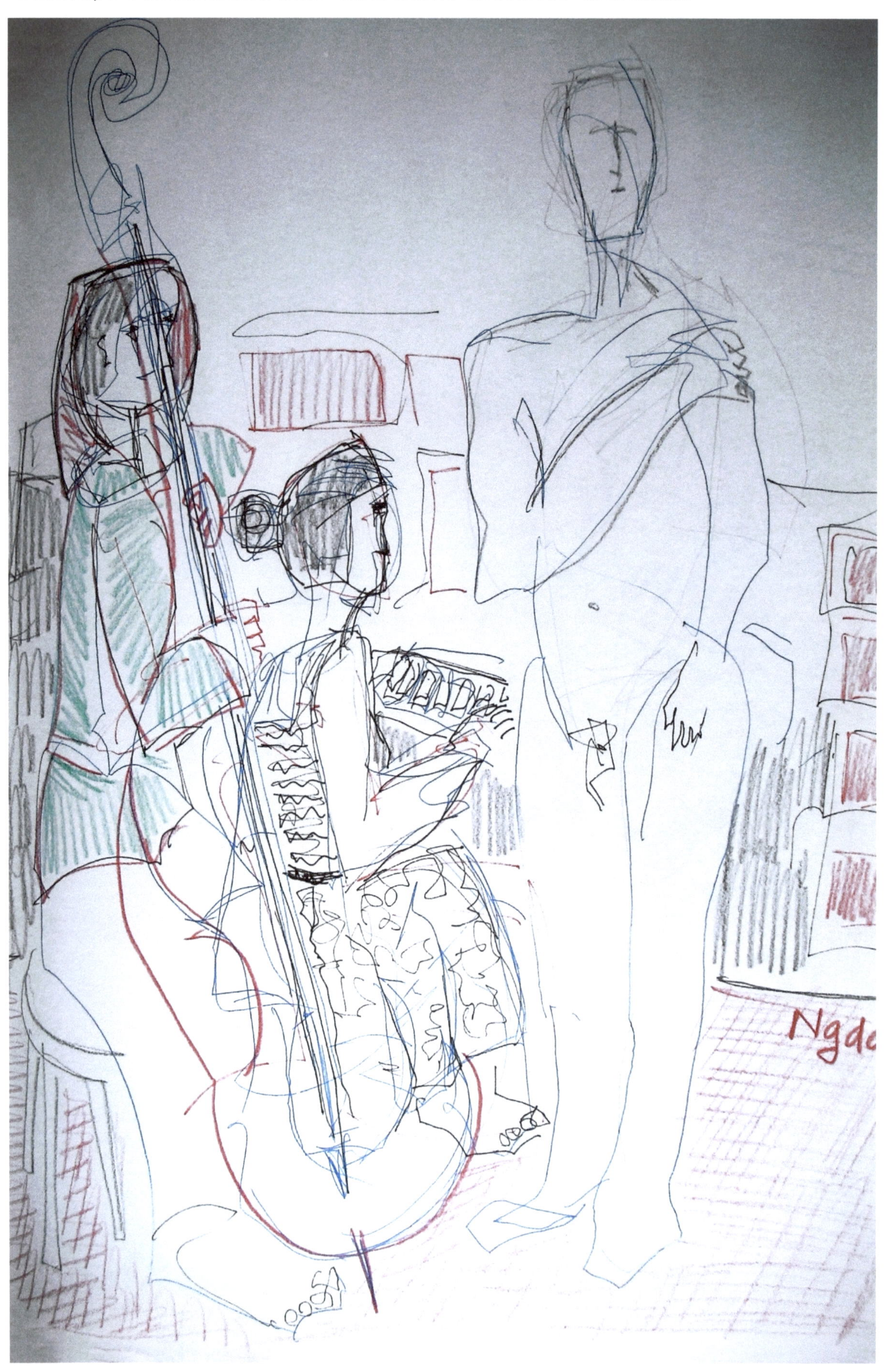
Ngd

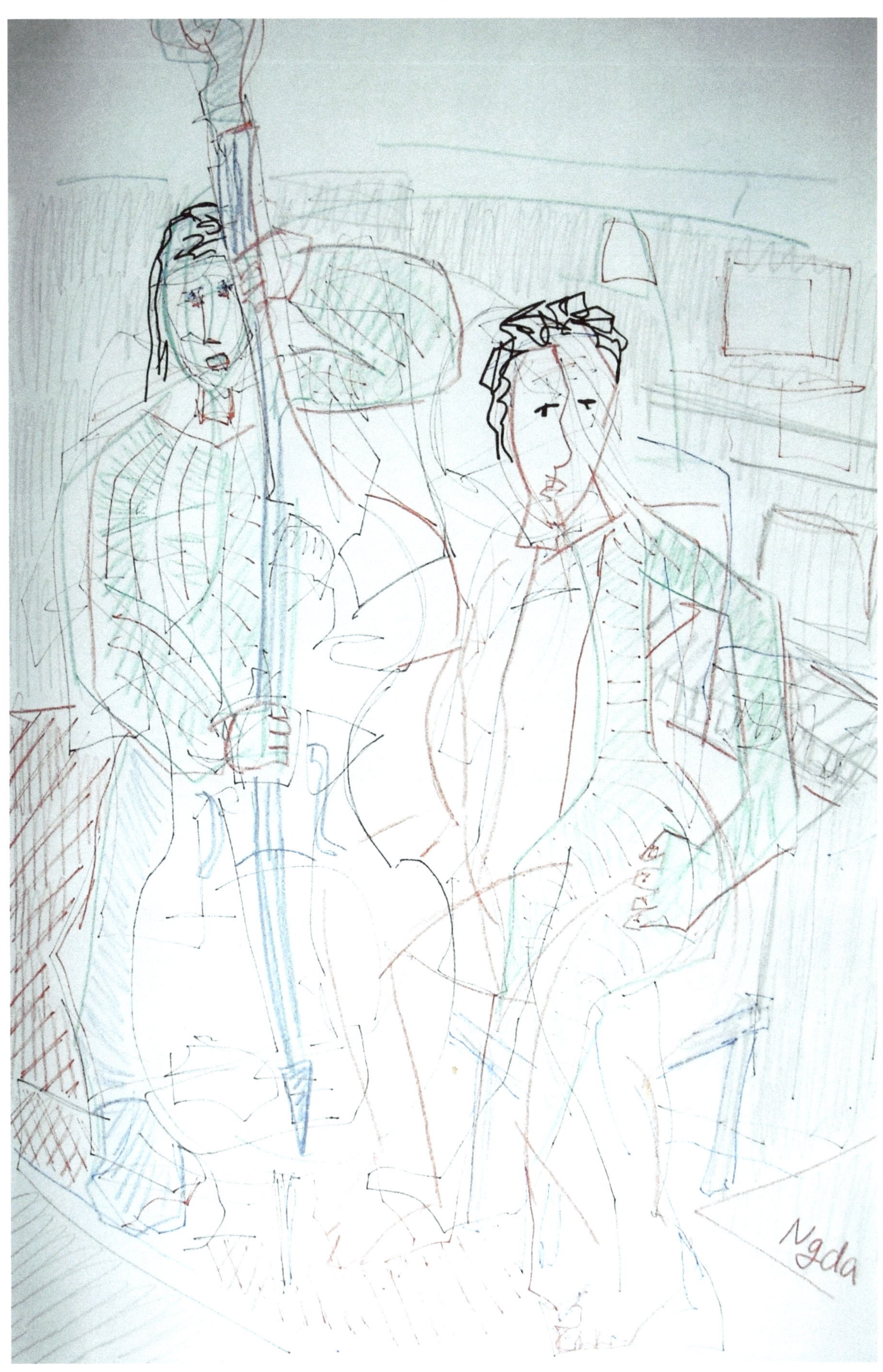

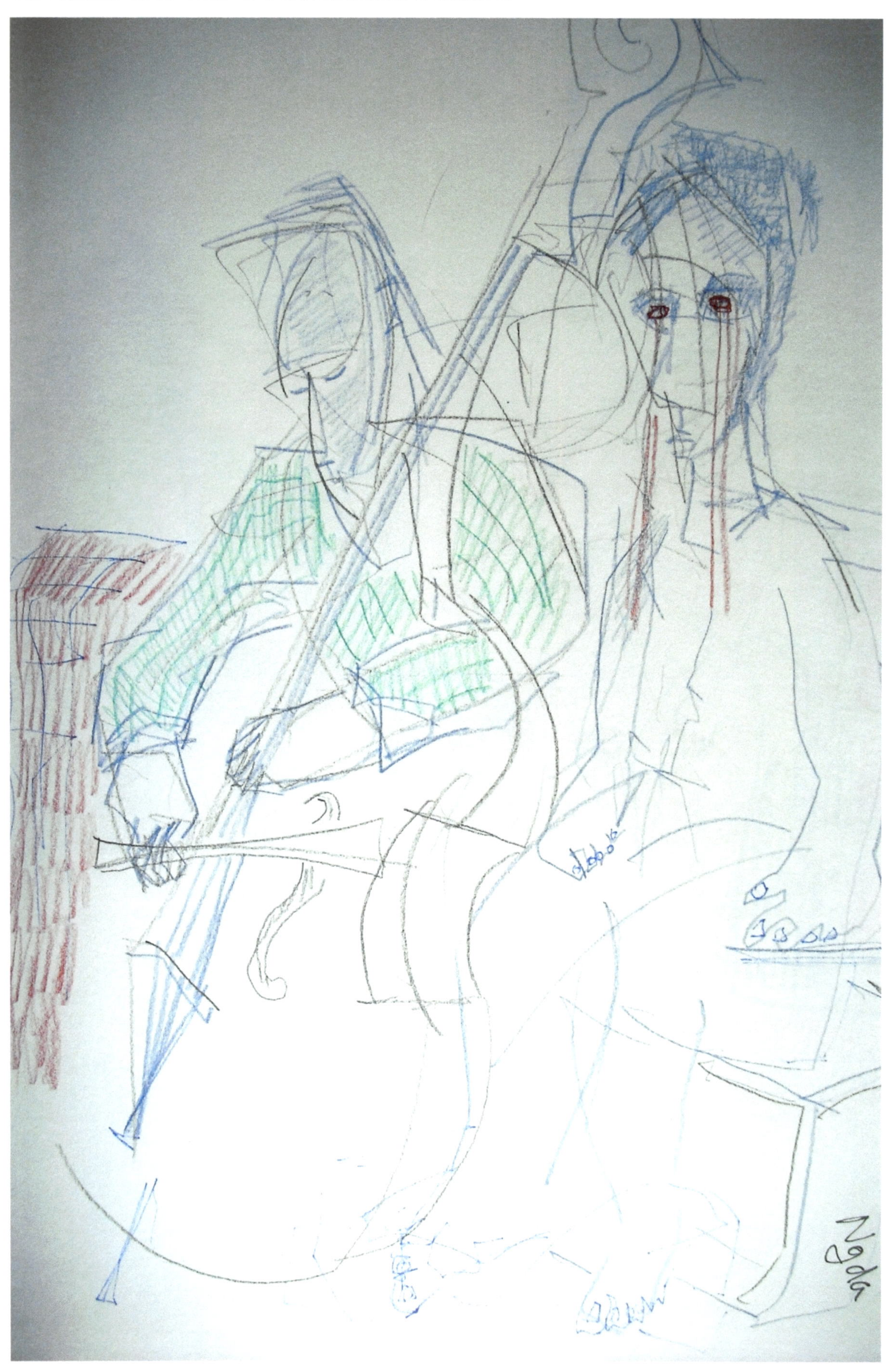

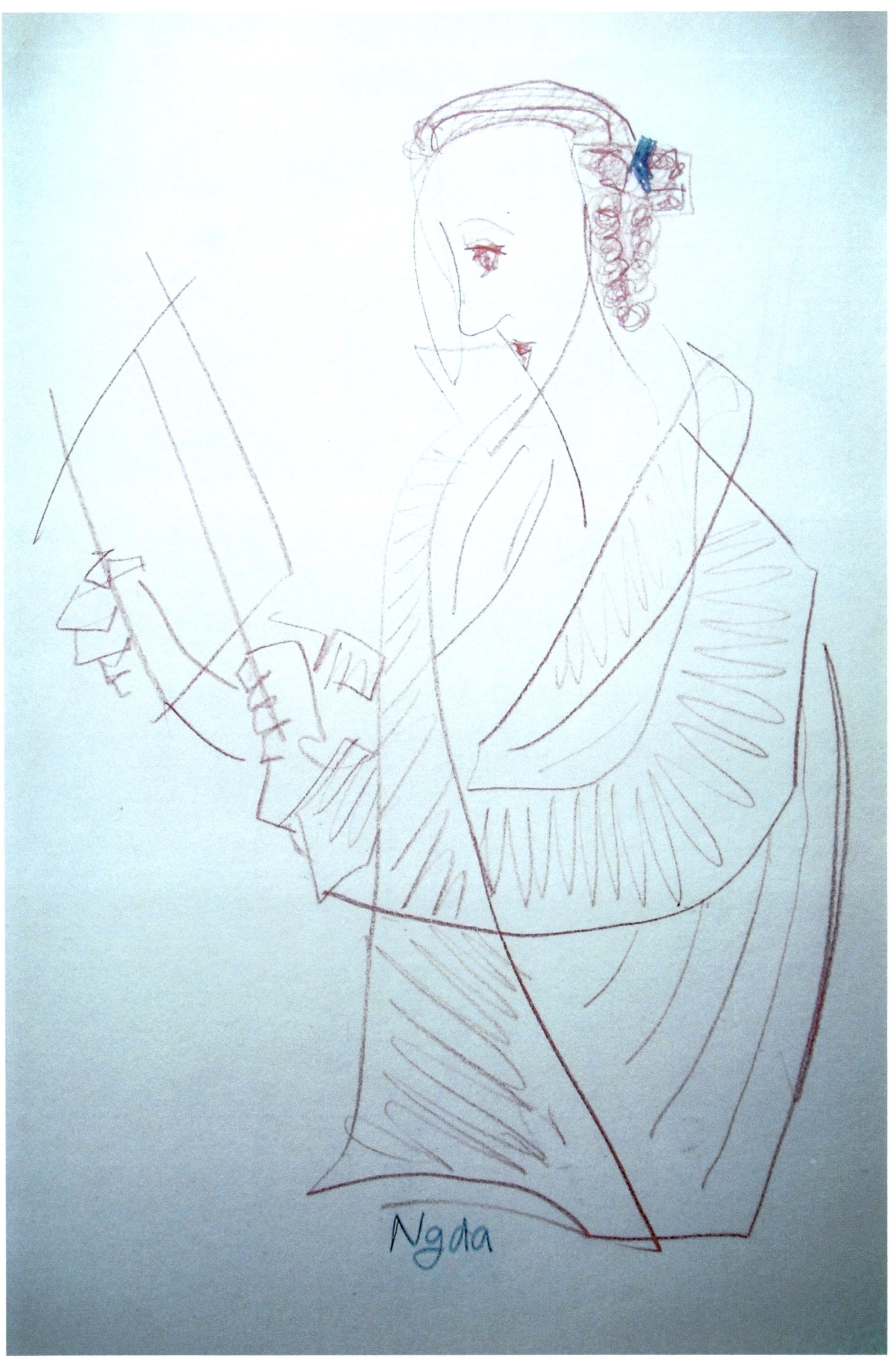
Ngda

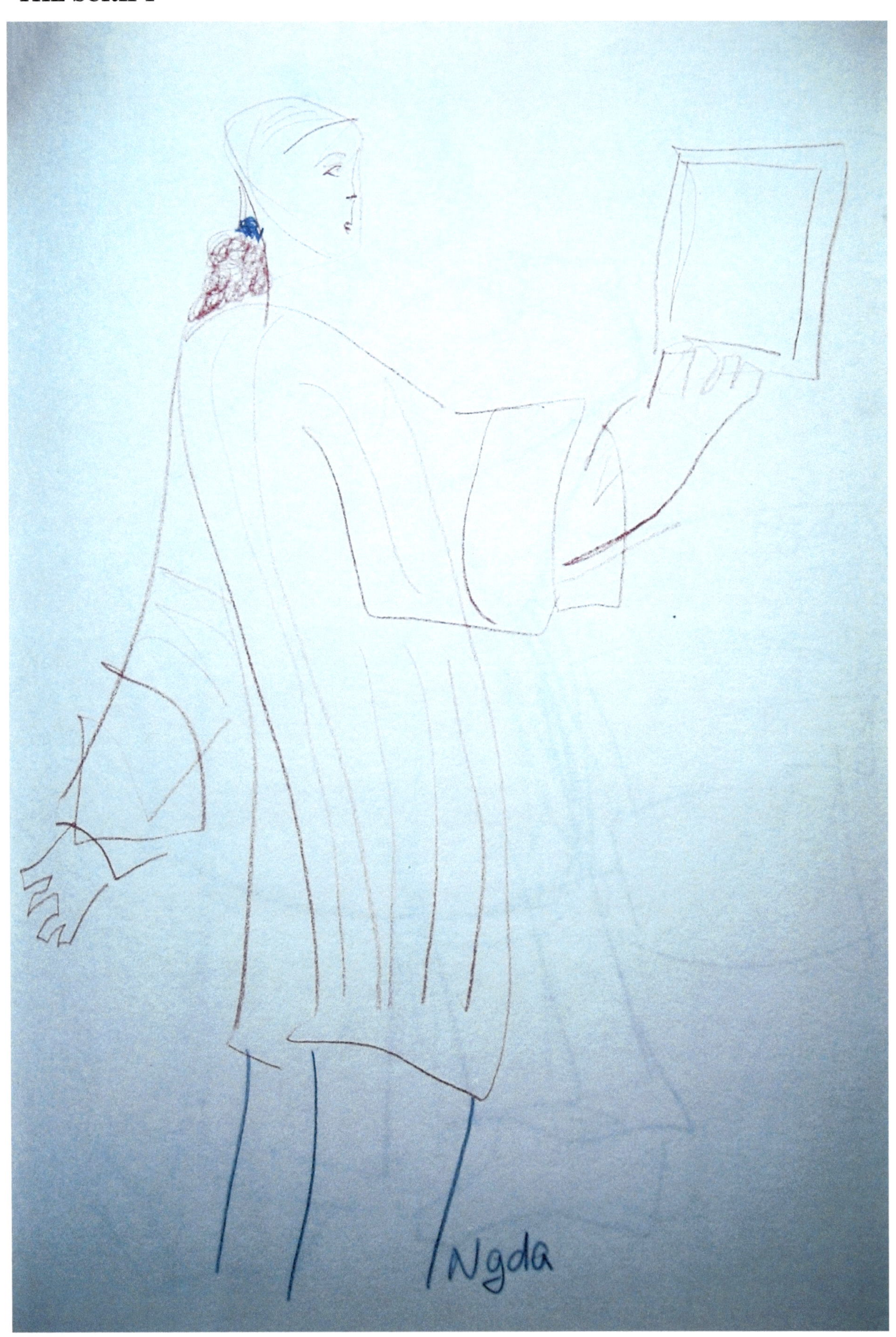

Ngda

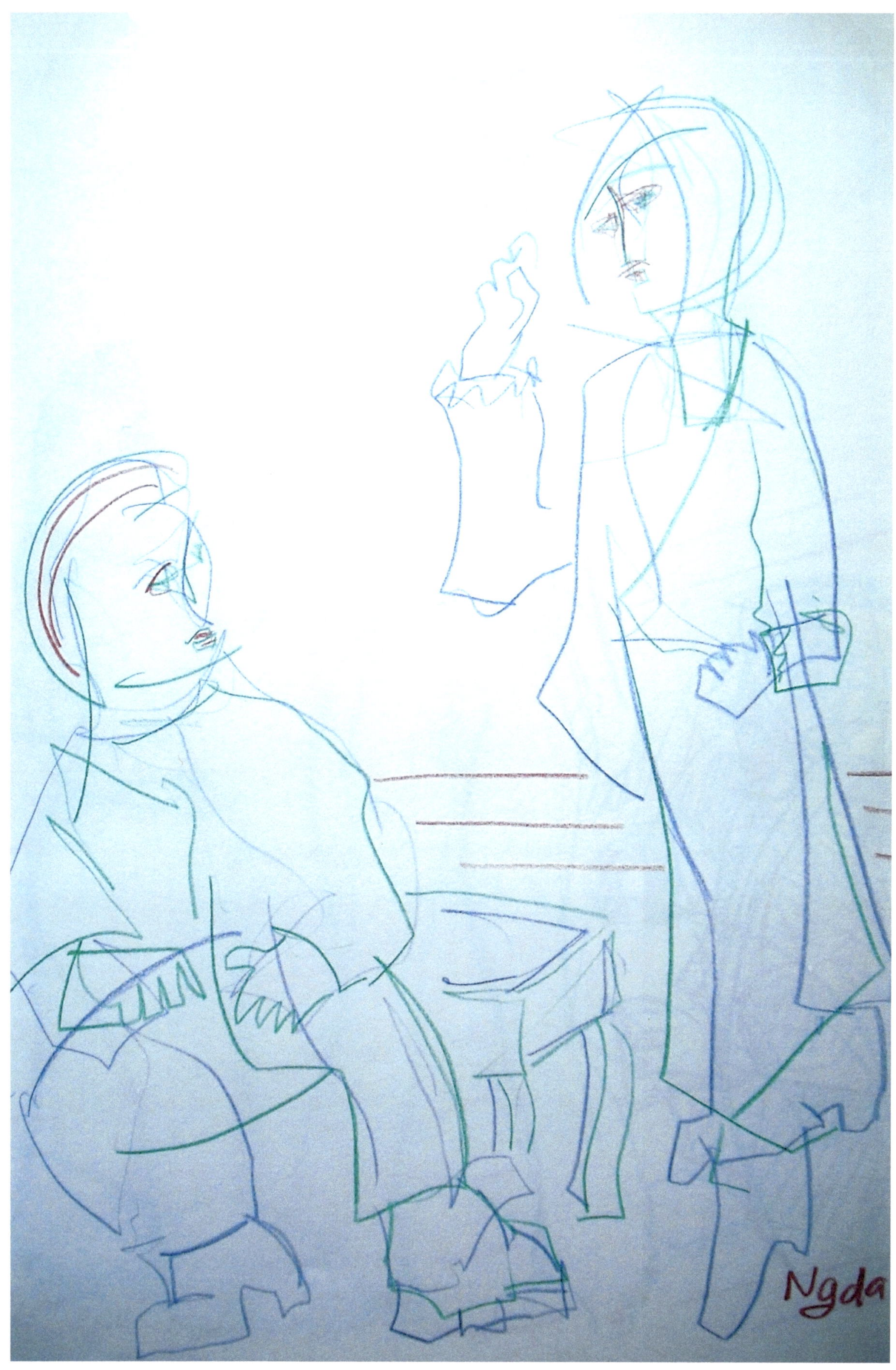
Ngda

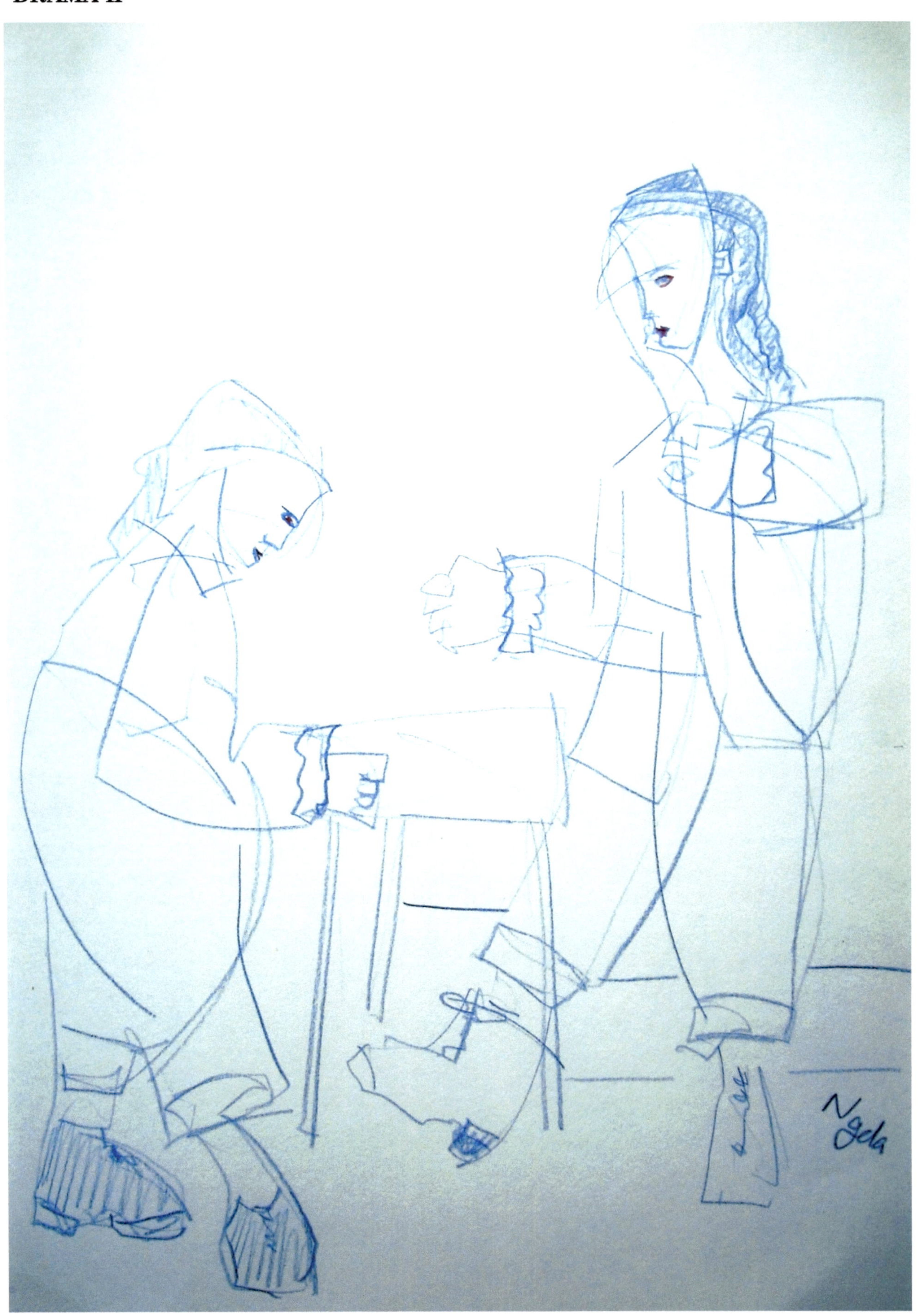

Najda in Line

"Gedankenexperiemnt"

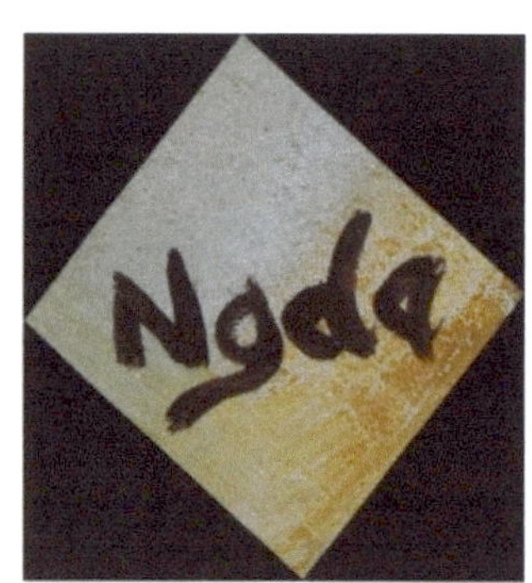

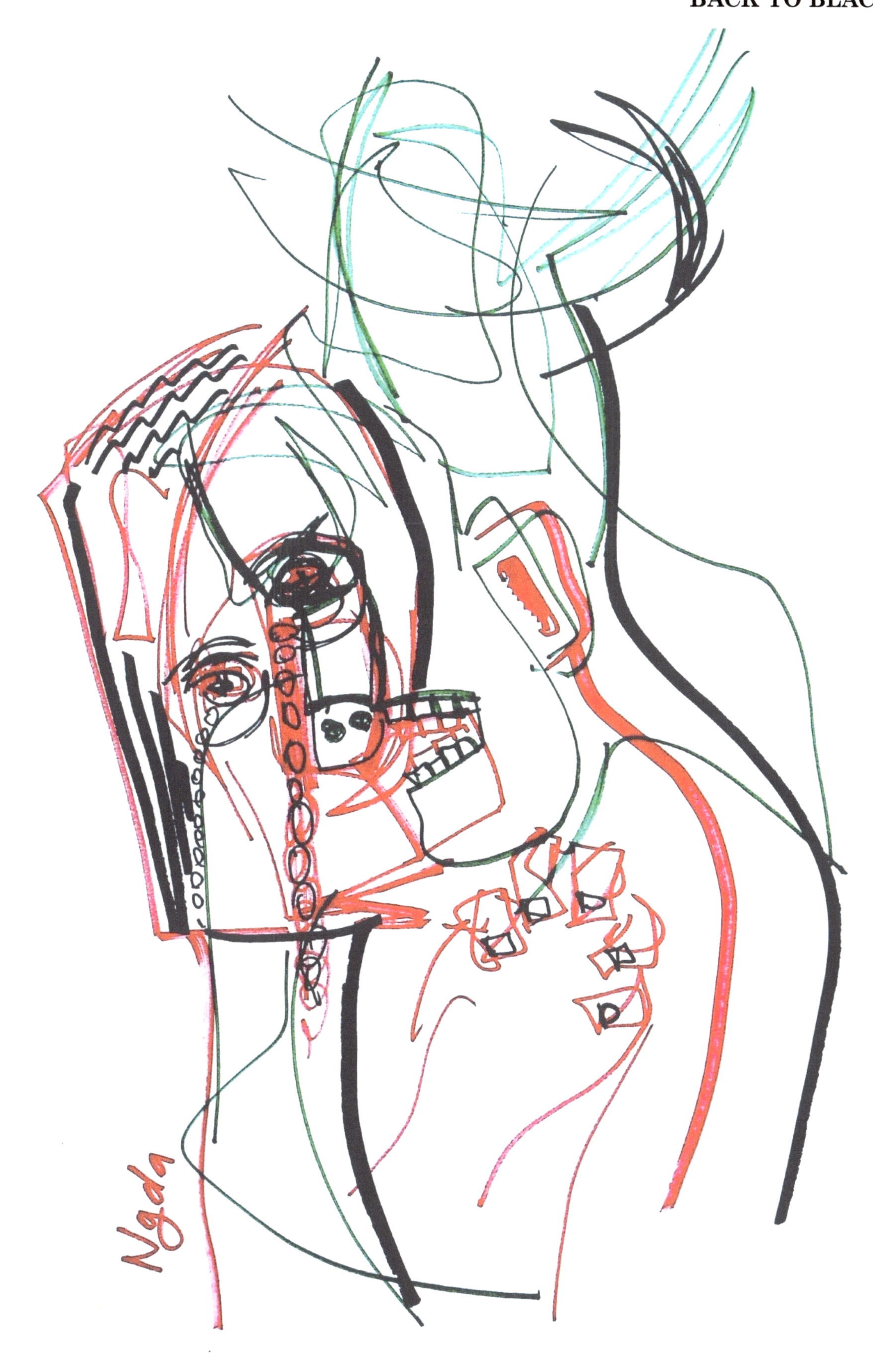

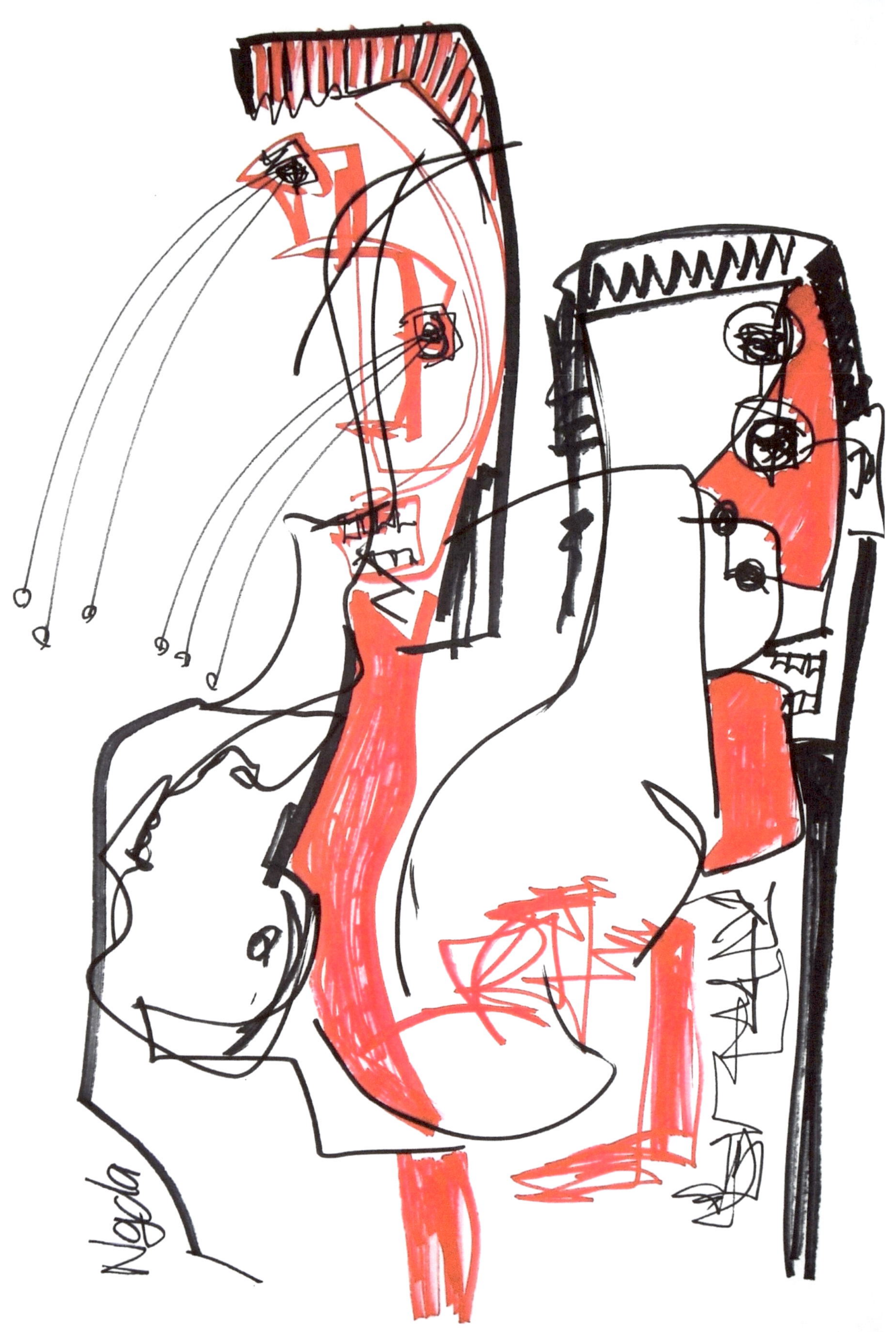

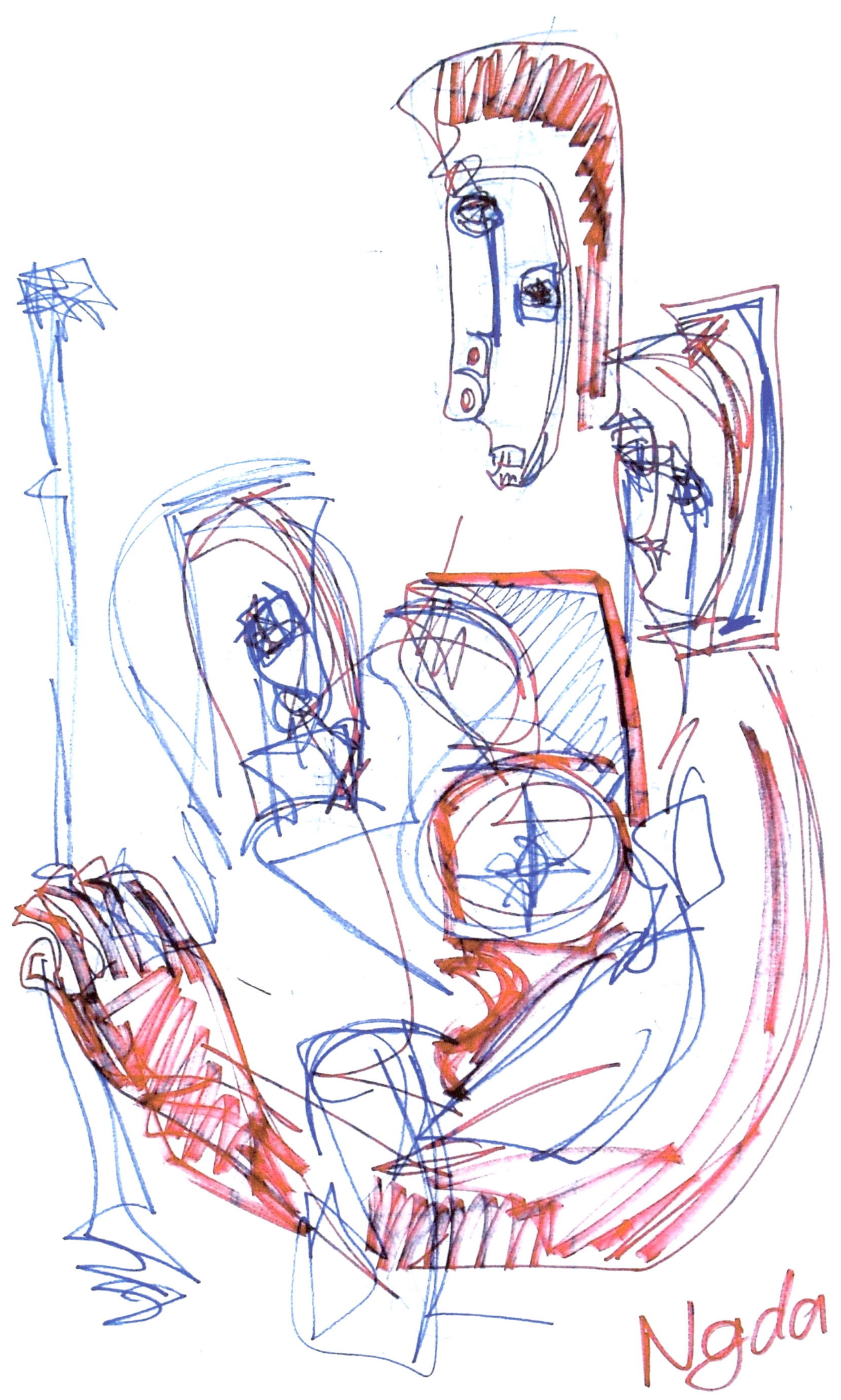

"THE INNOCENTS"

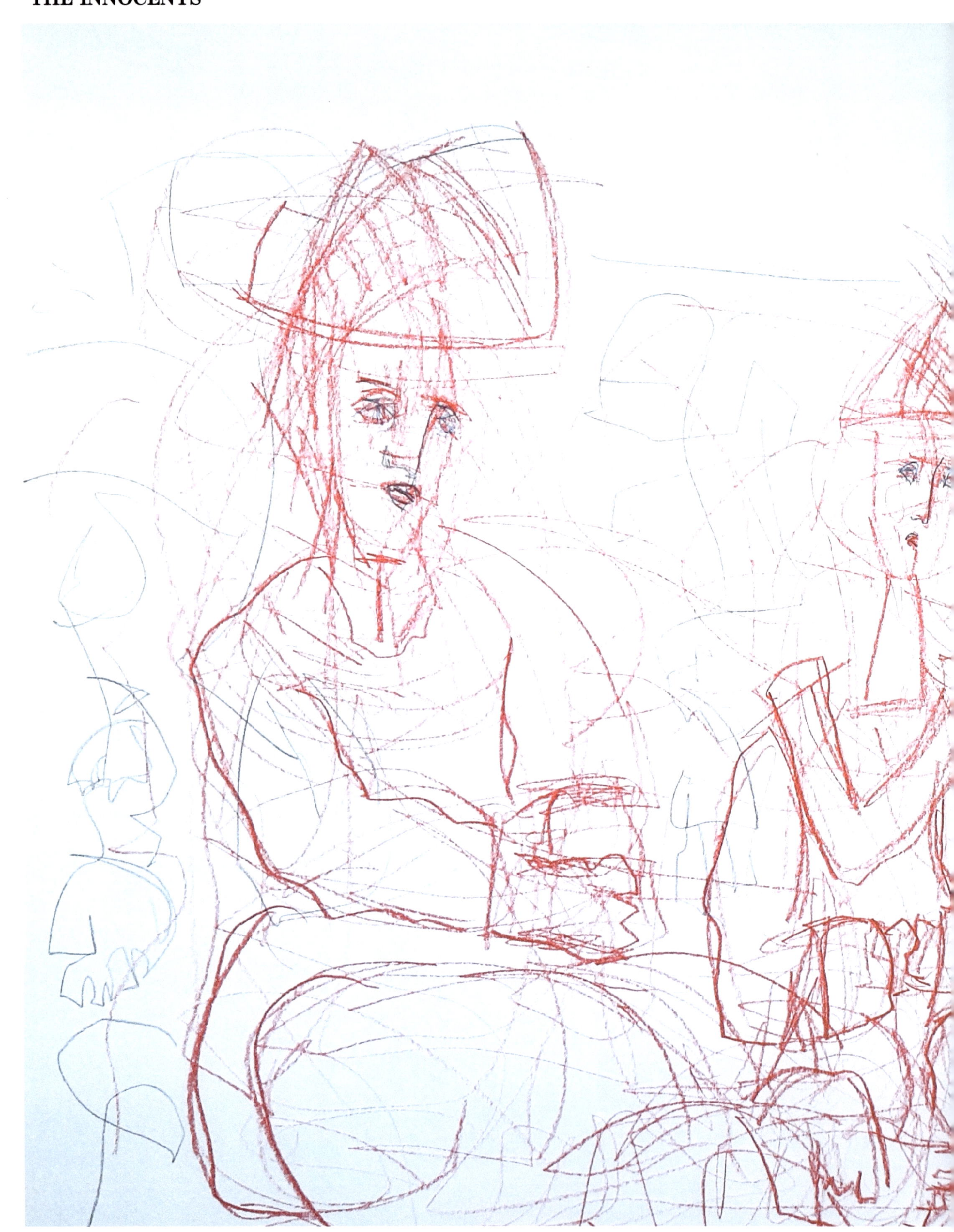

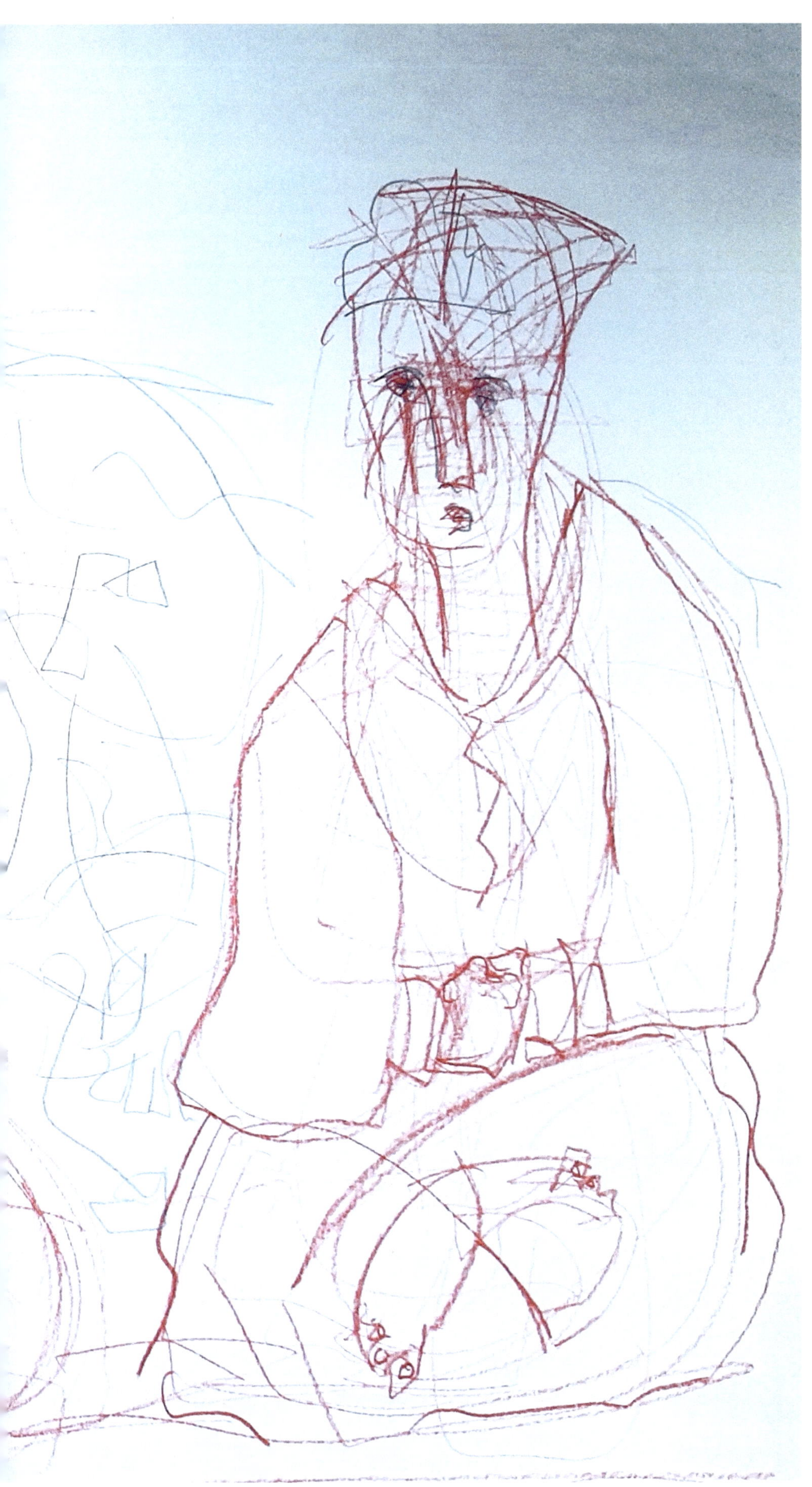

“THE HURTING”

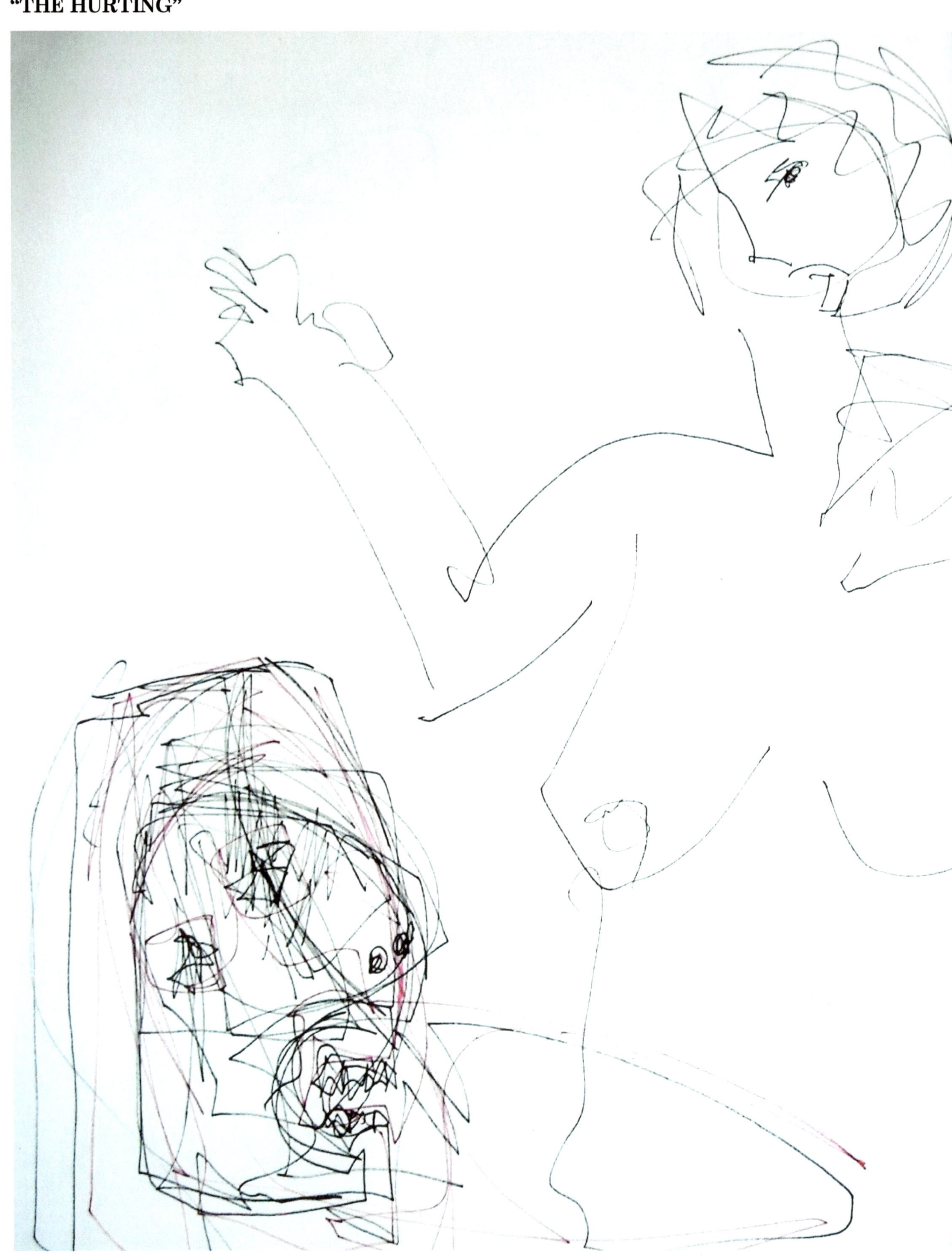

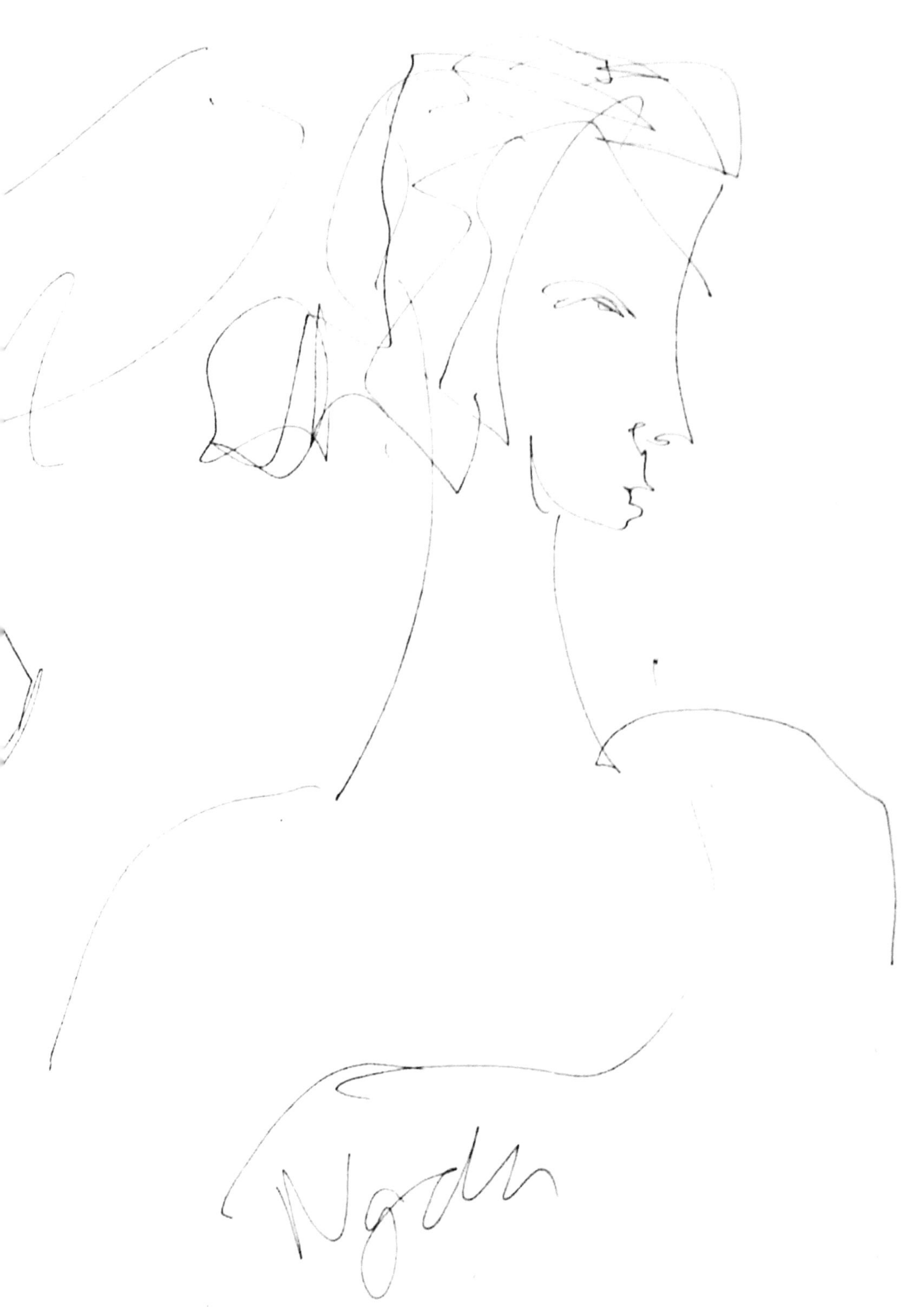

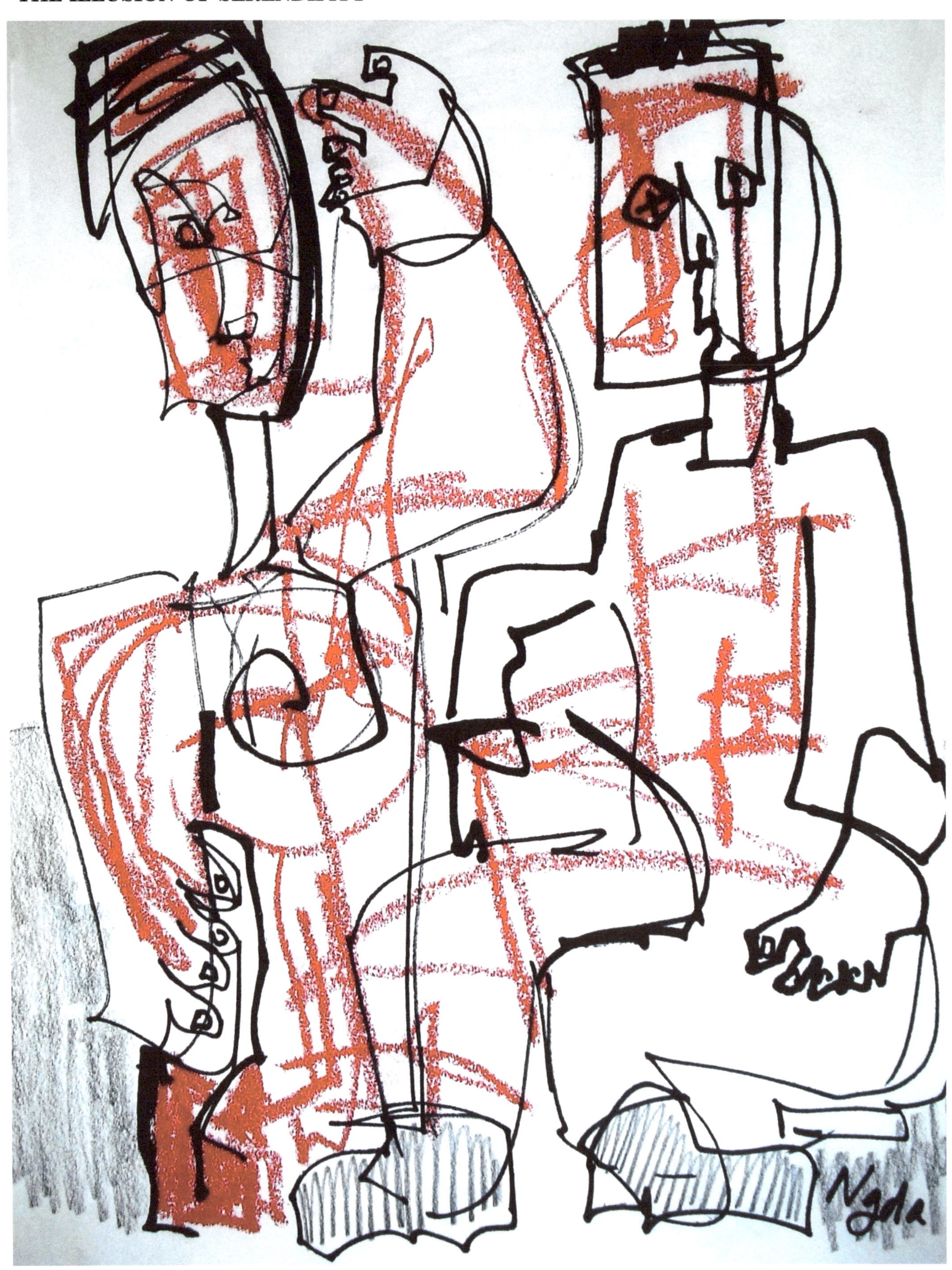

Najda in Line

"Portrait"

Agora Gallery

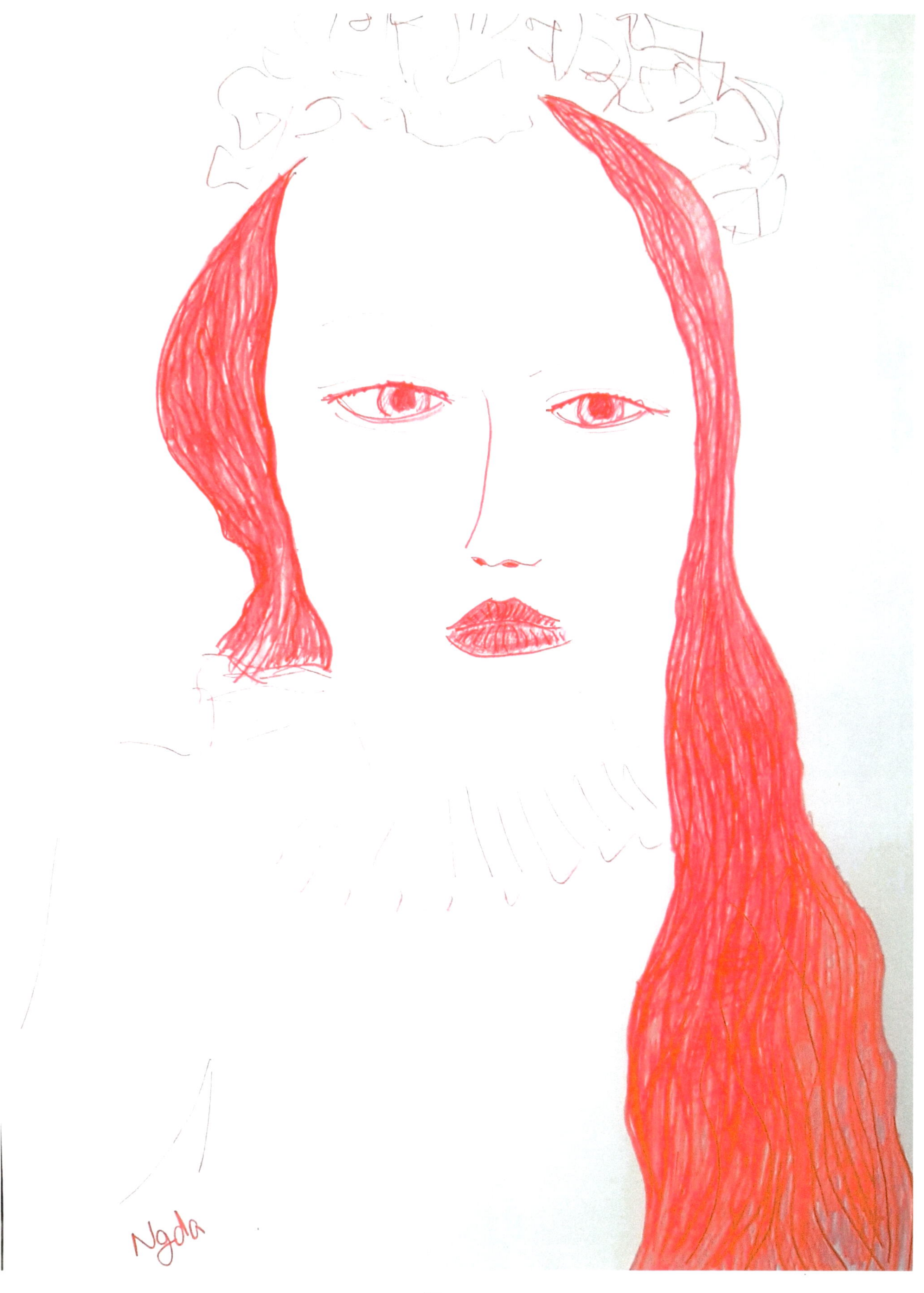

"KOTI & OLGA"

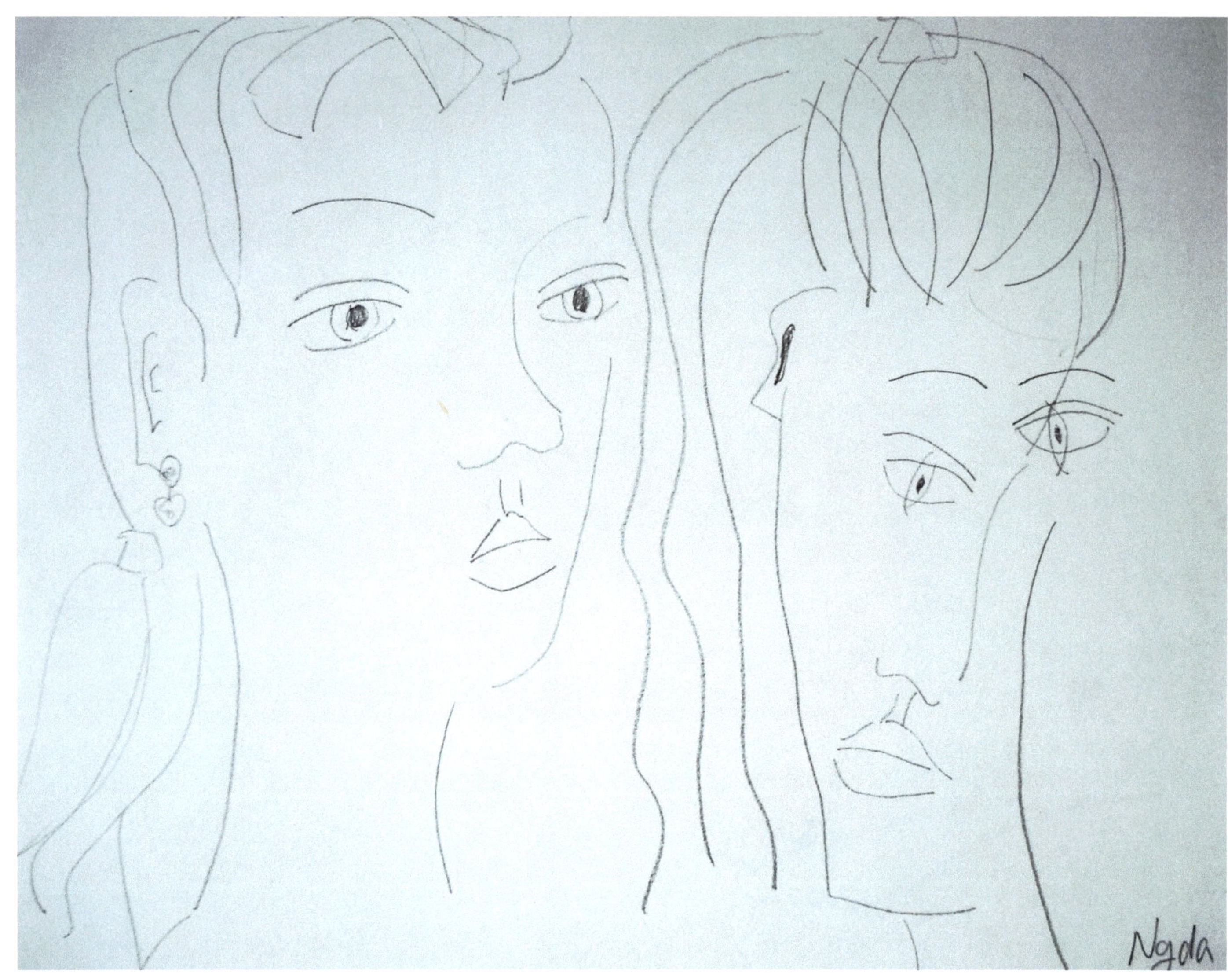

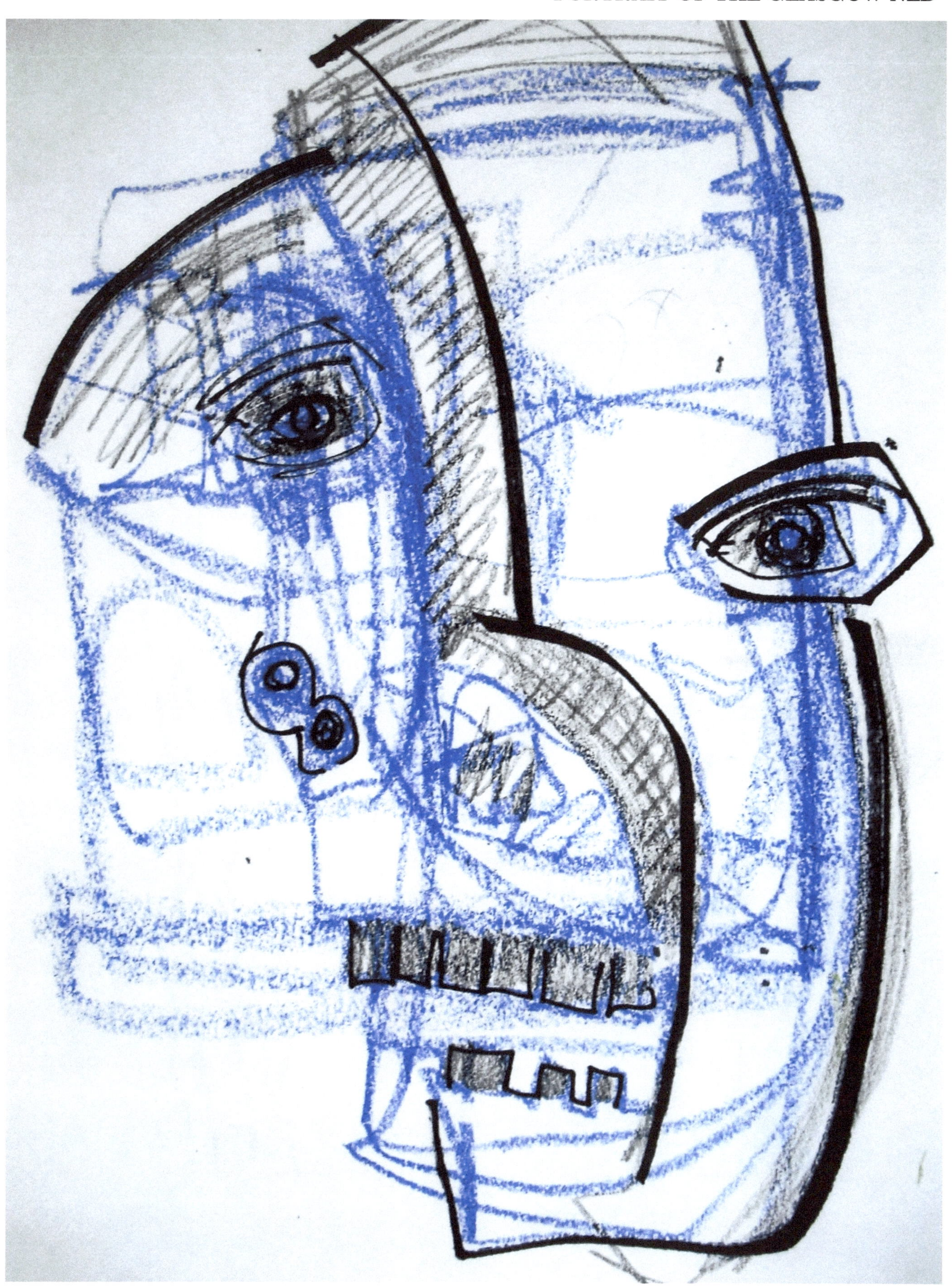

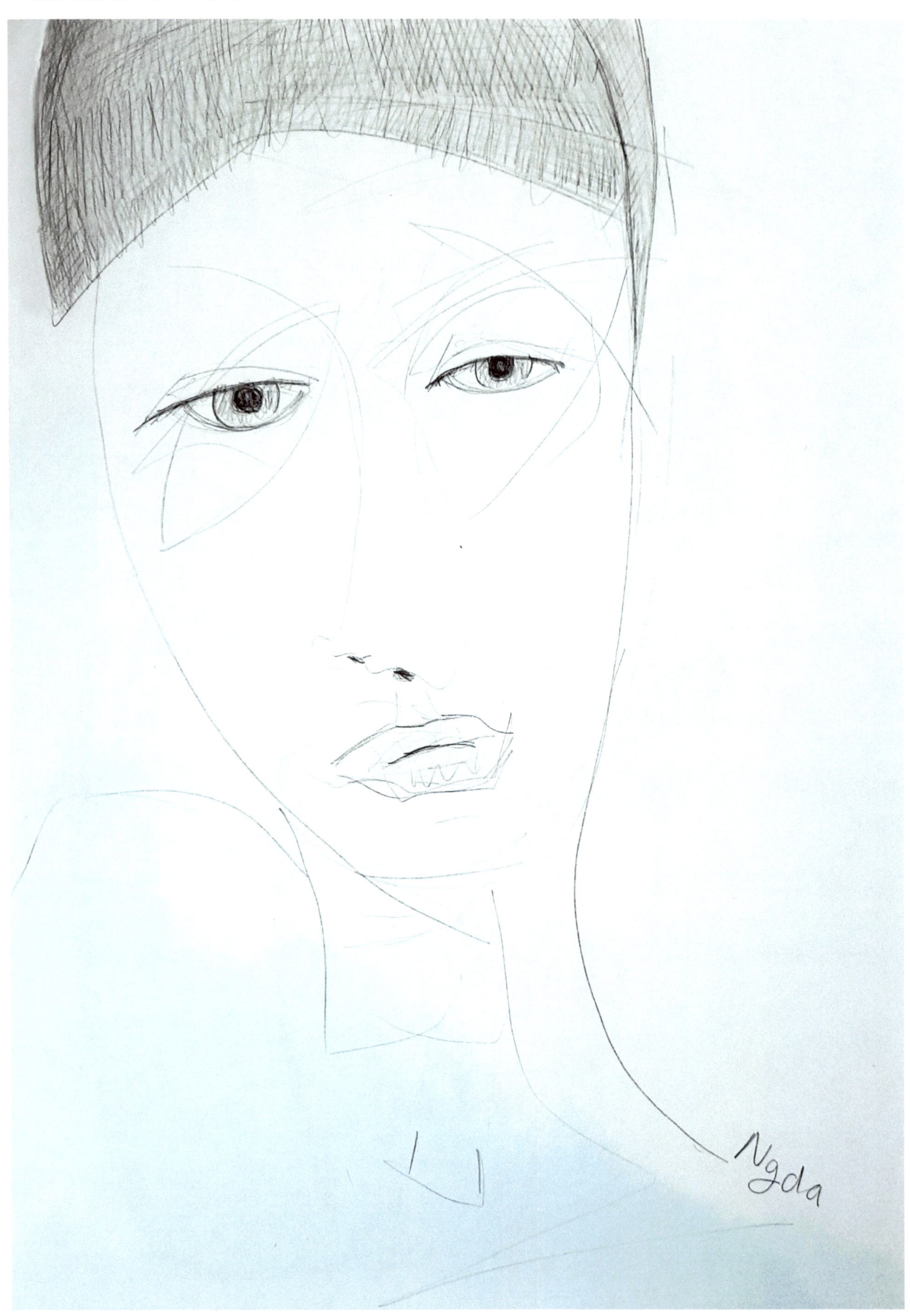

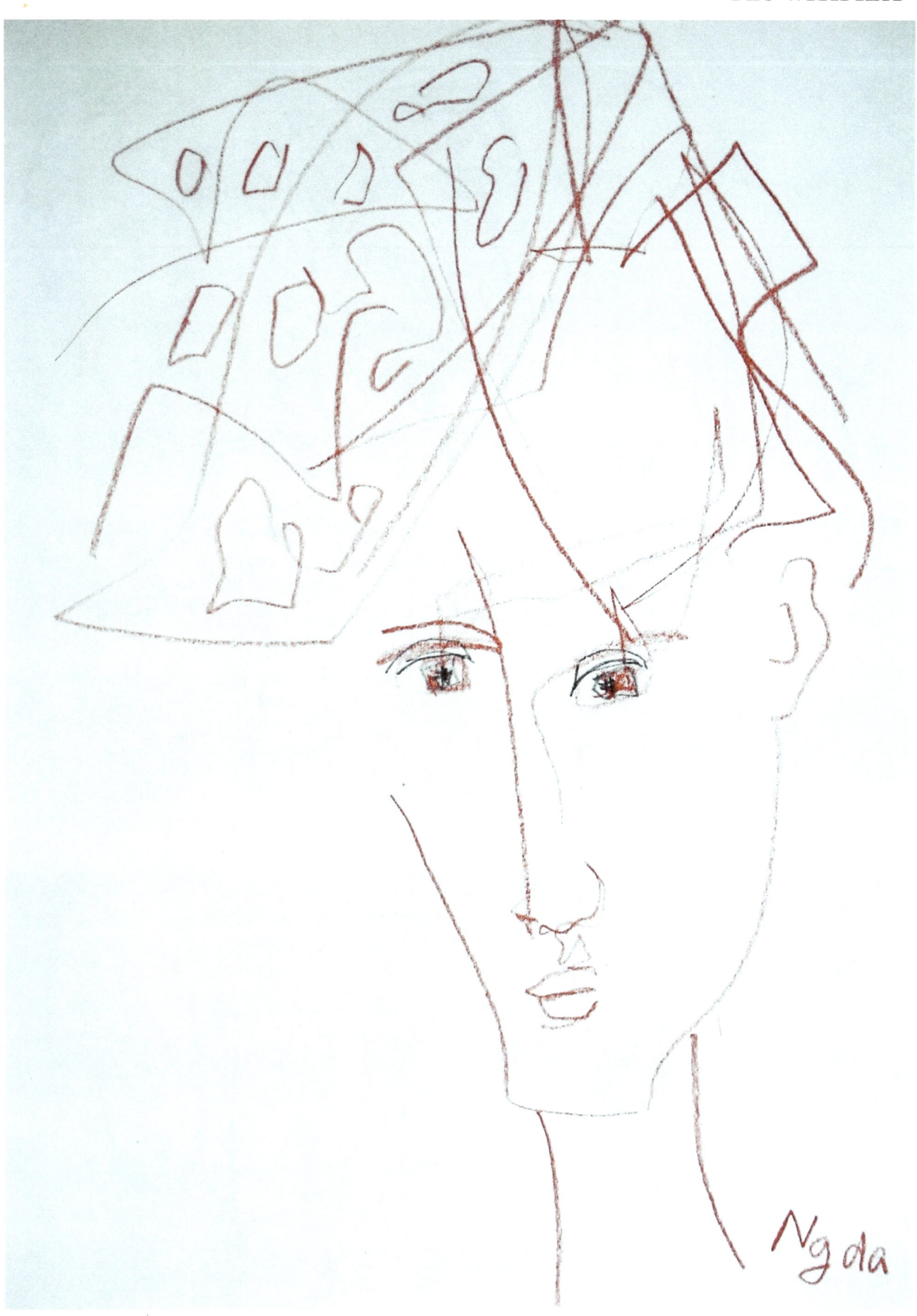

"MORGAN"

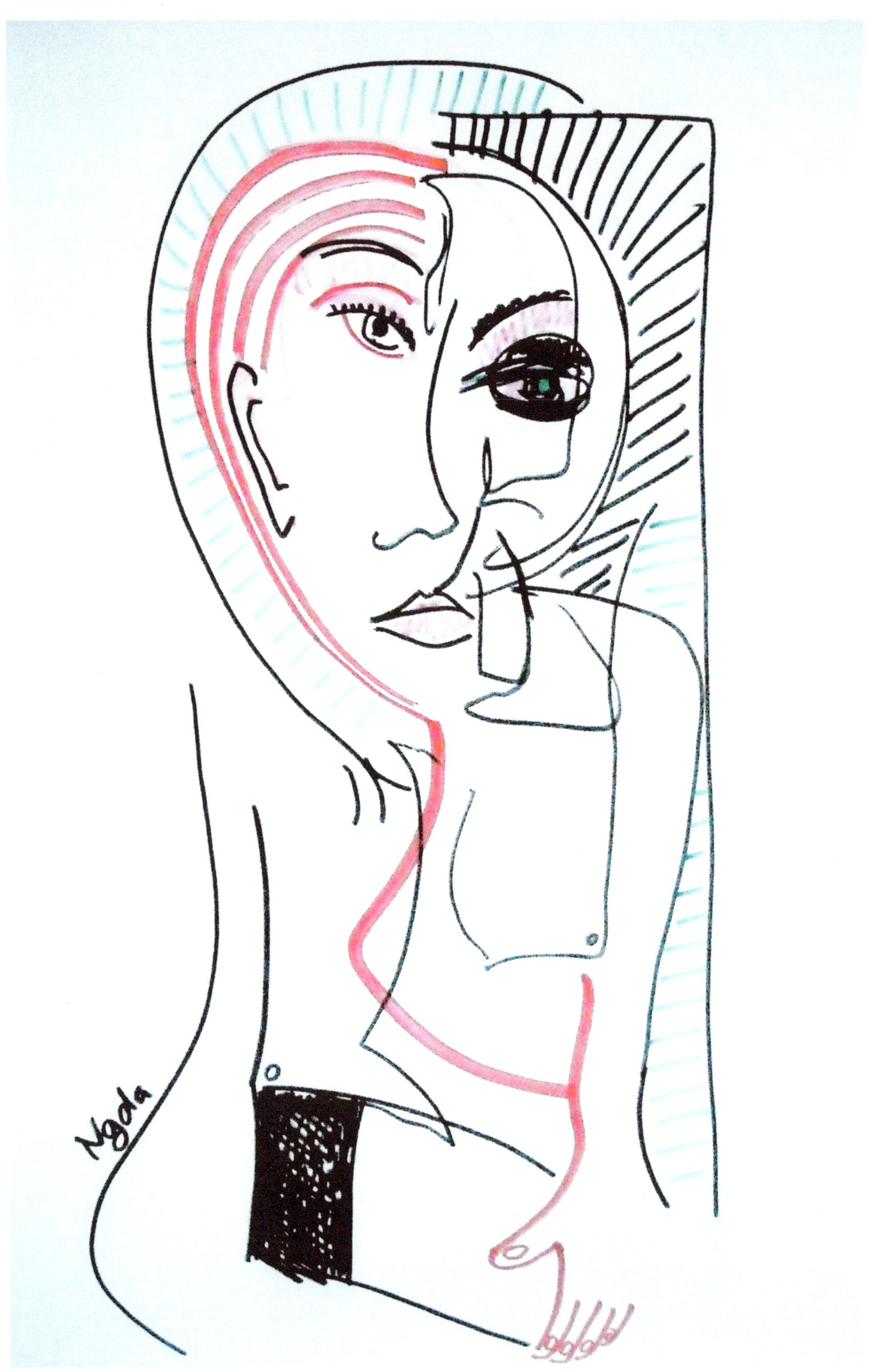

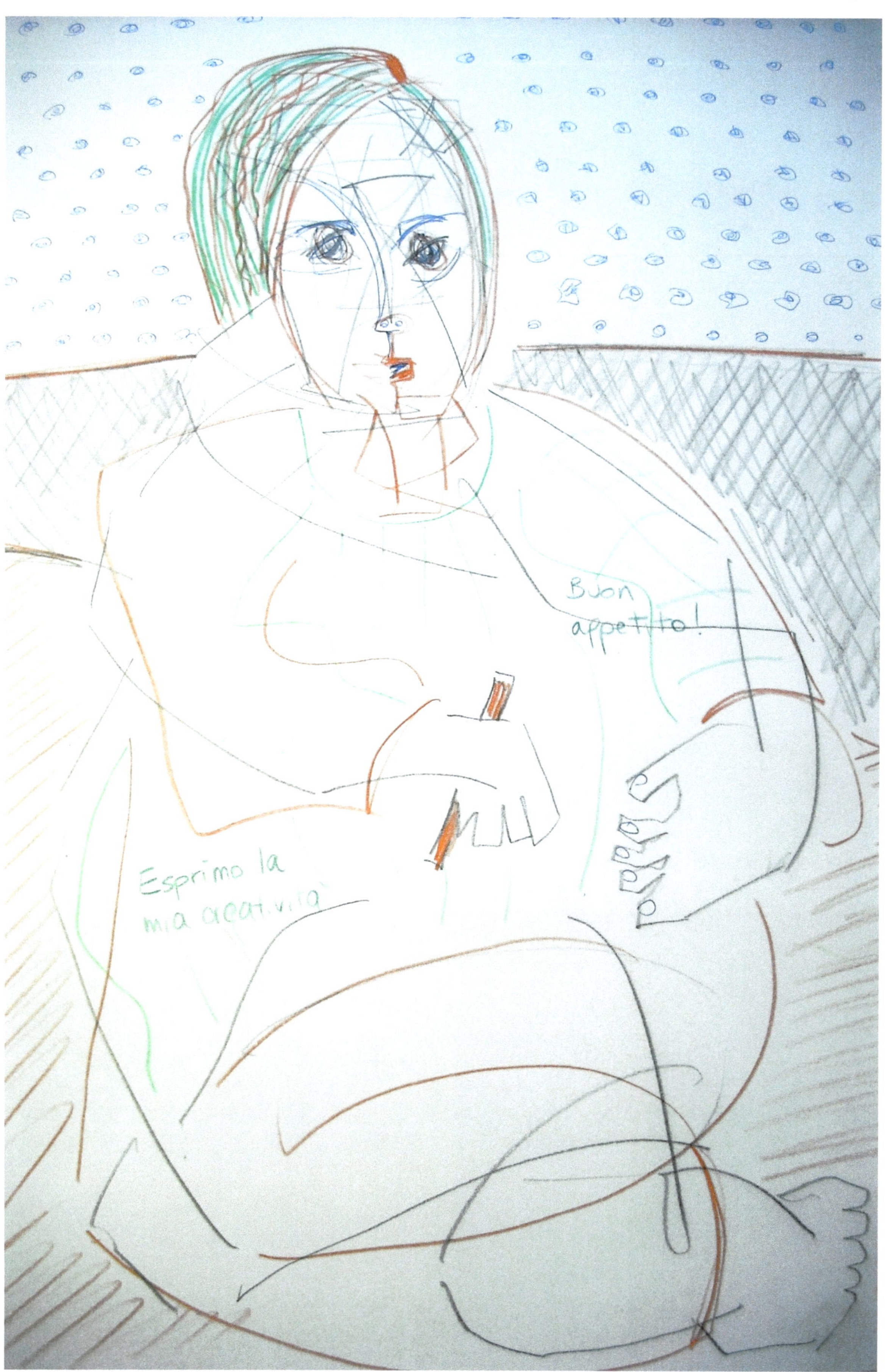
Buon
appetito!
Esprimo la
mia creatività

"EWELINA"

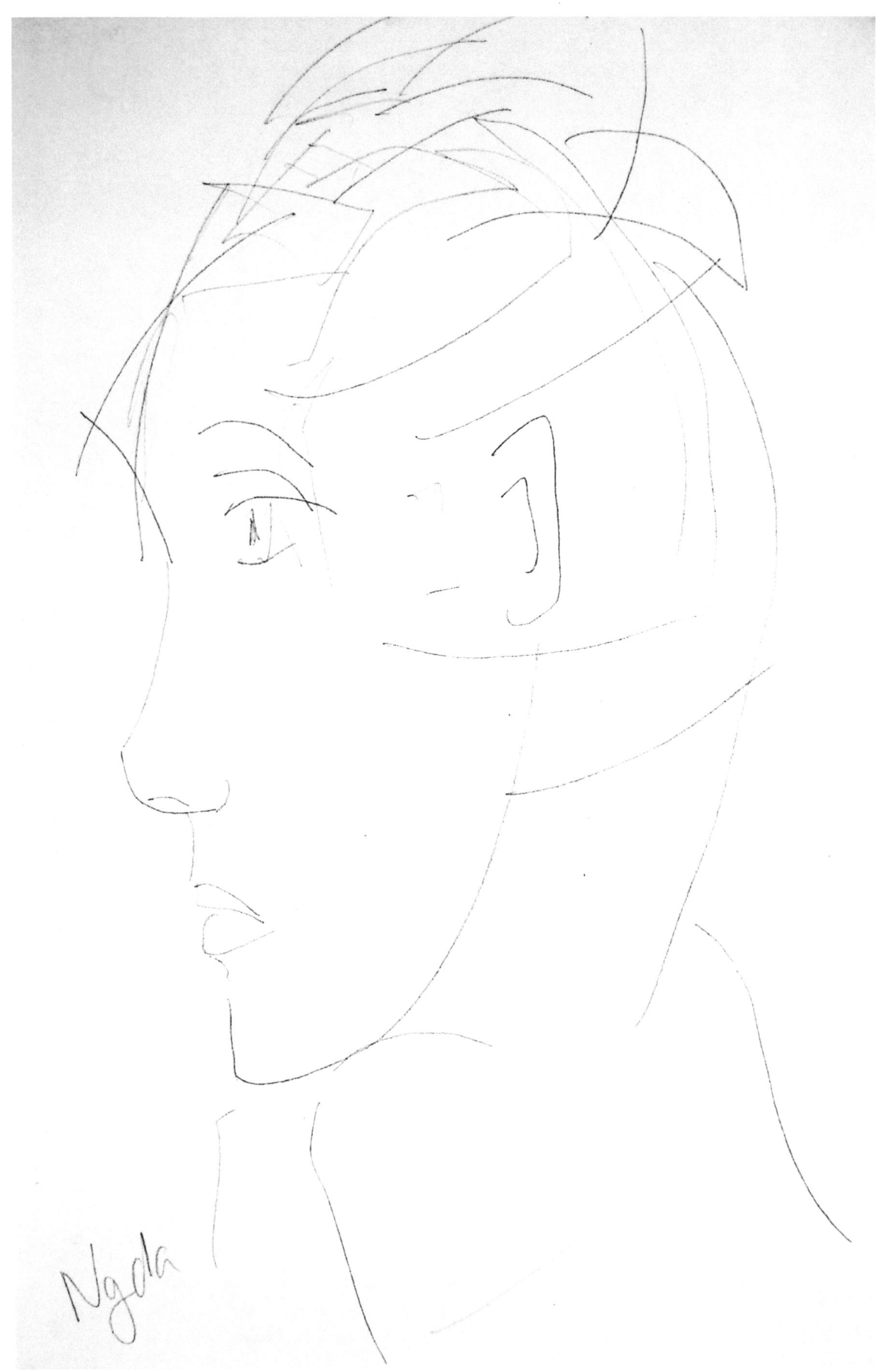

Najda in Line

"Life Room"

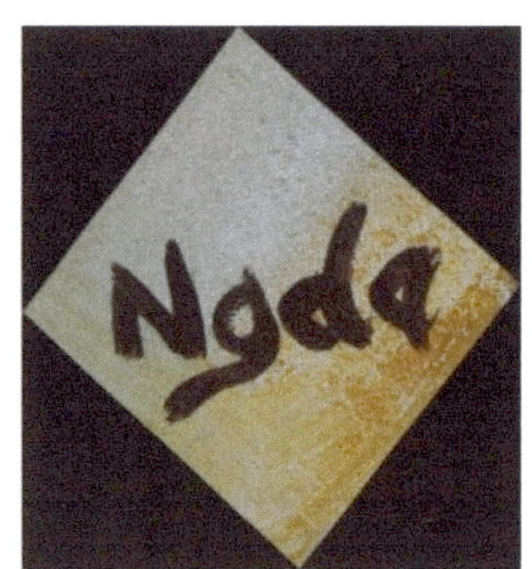

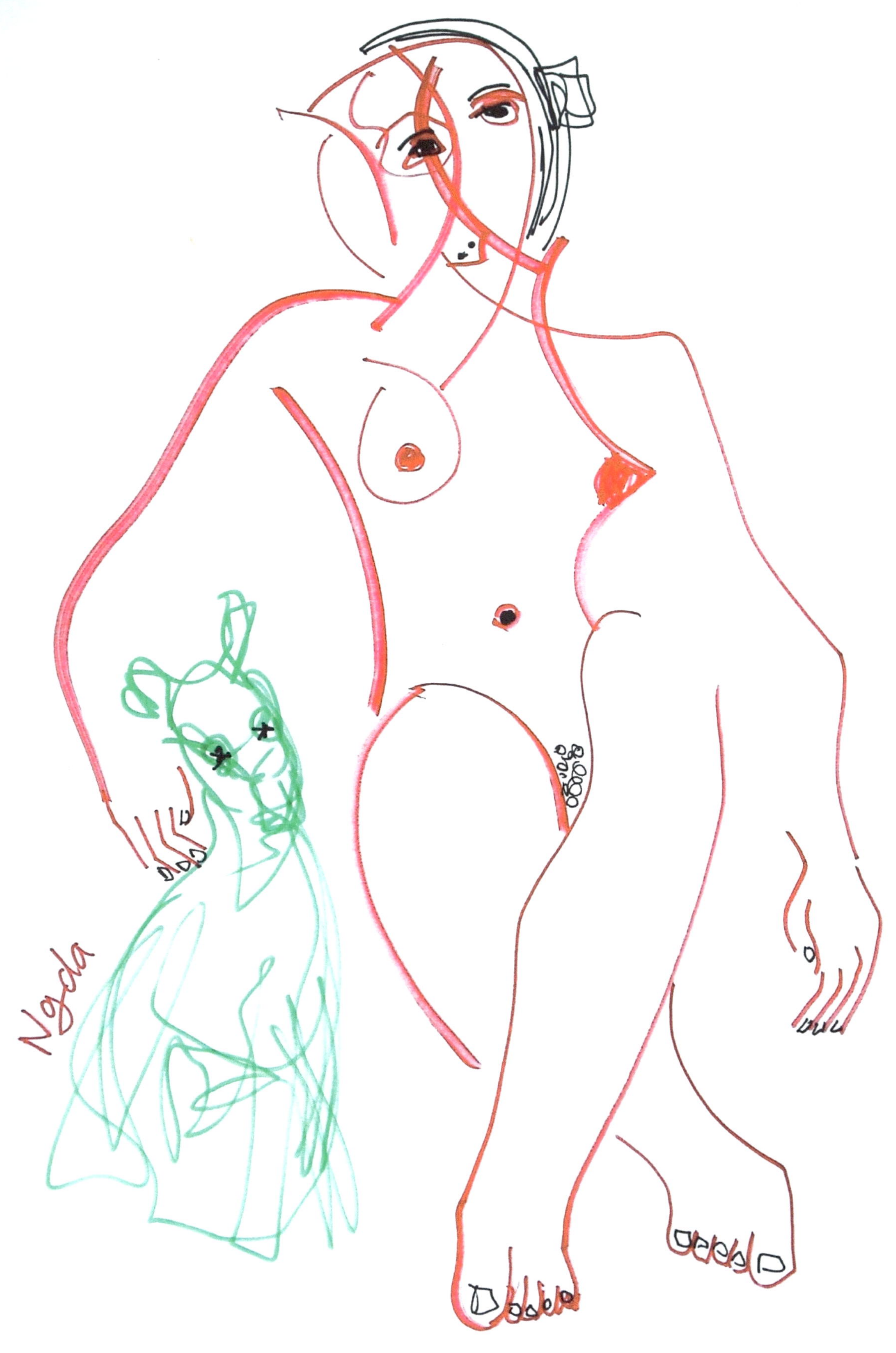

Ngda

"HANNA WITH NEW HAIRCUT"

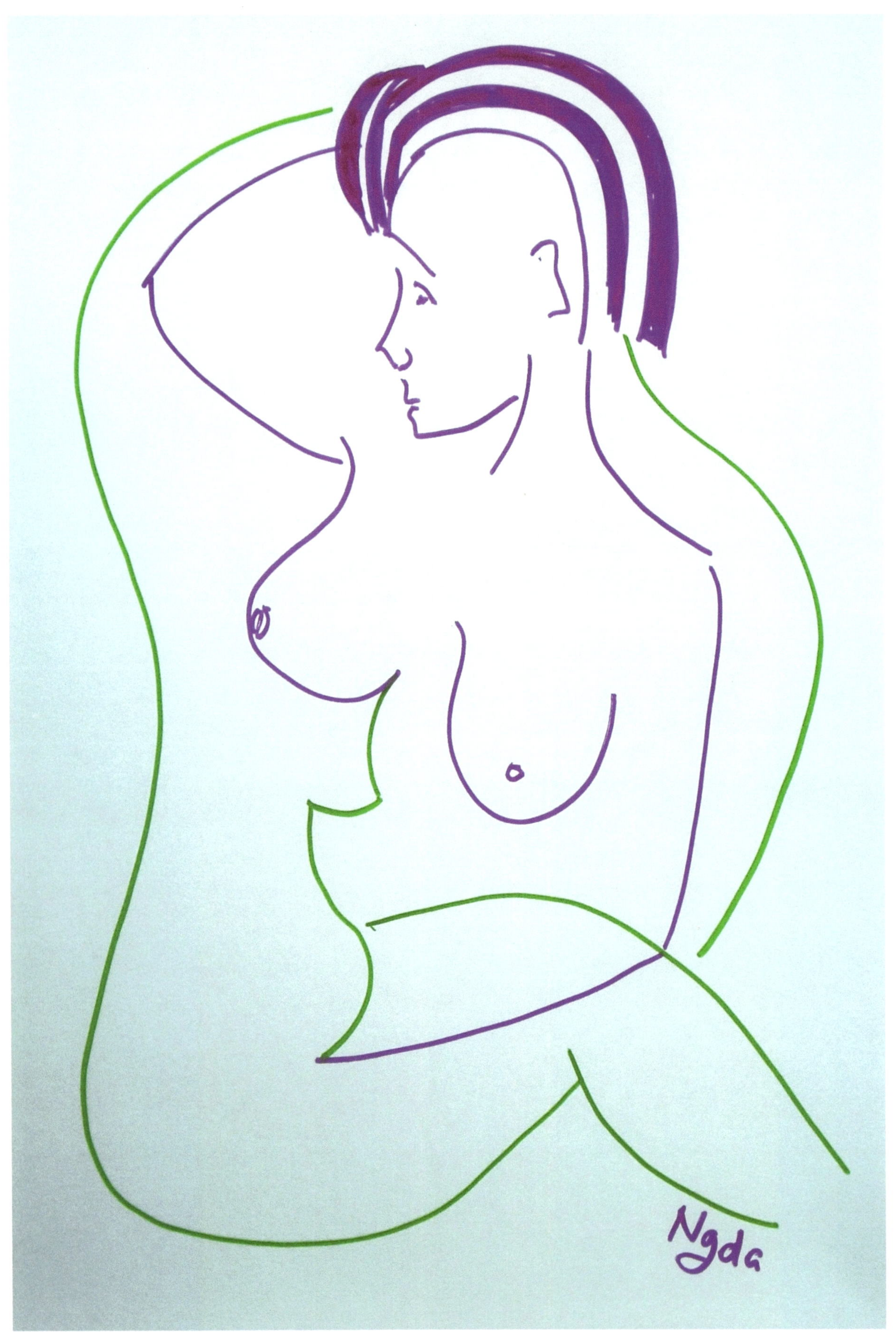

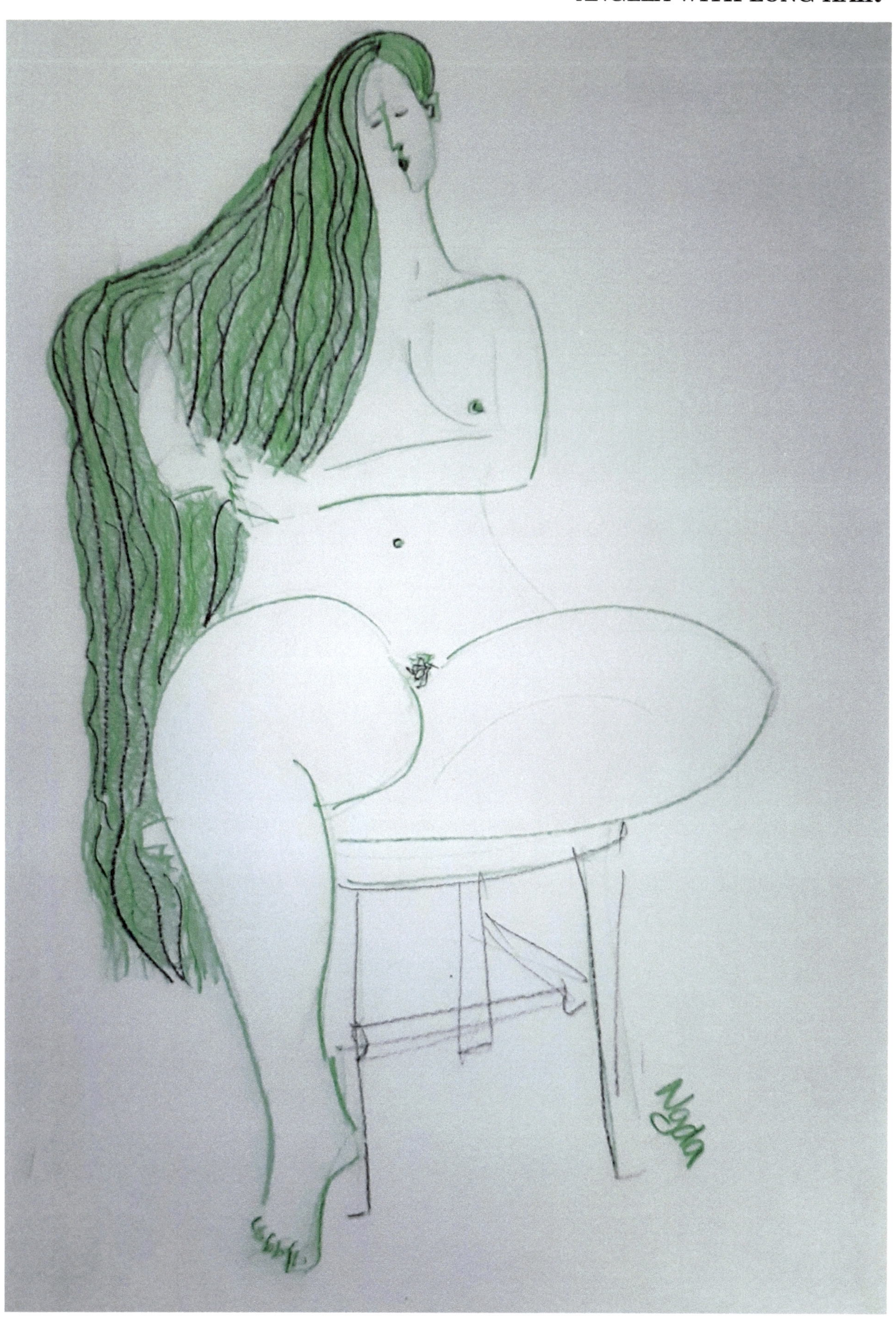

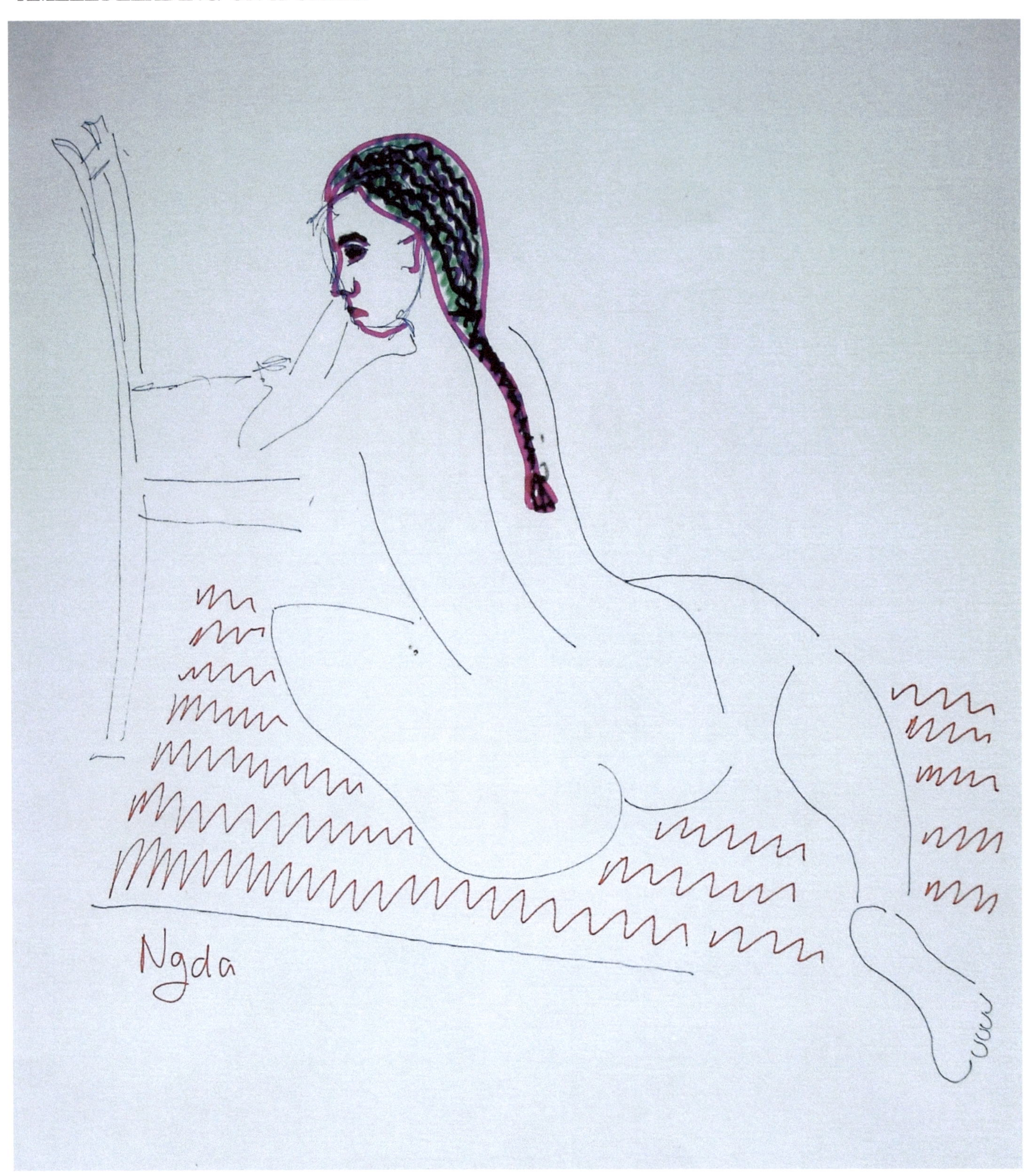
Ngda

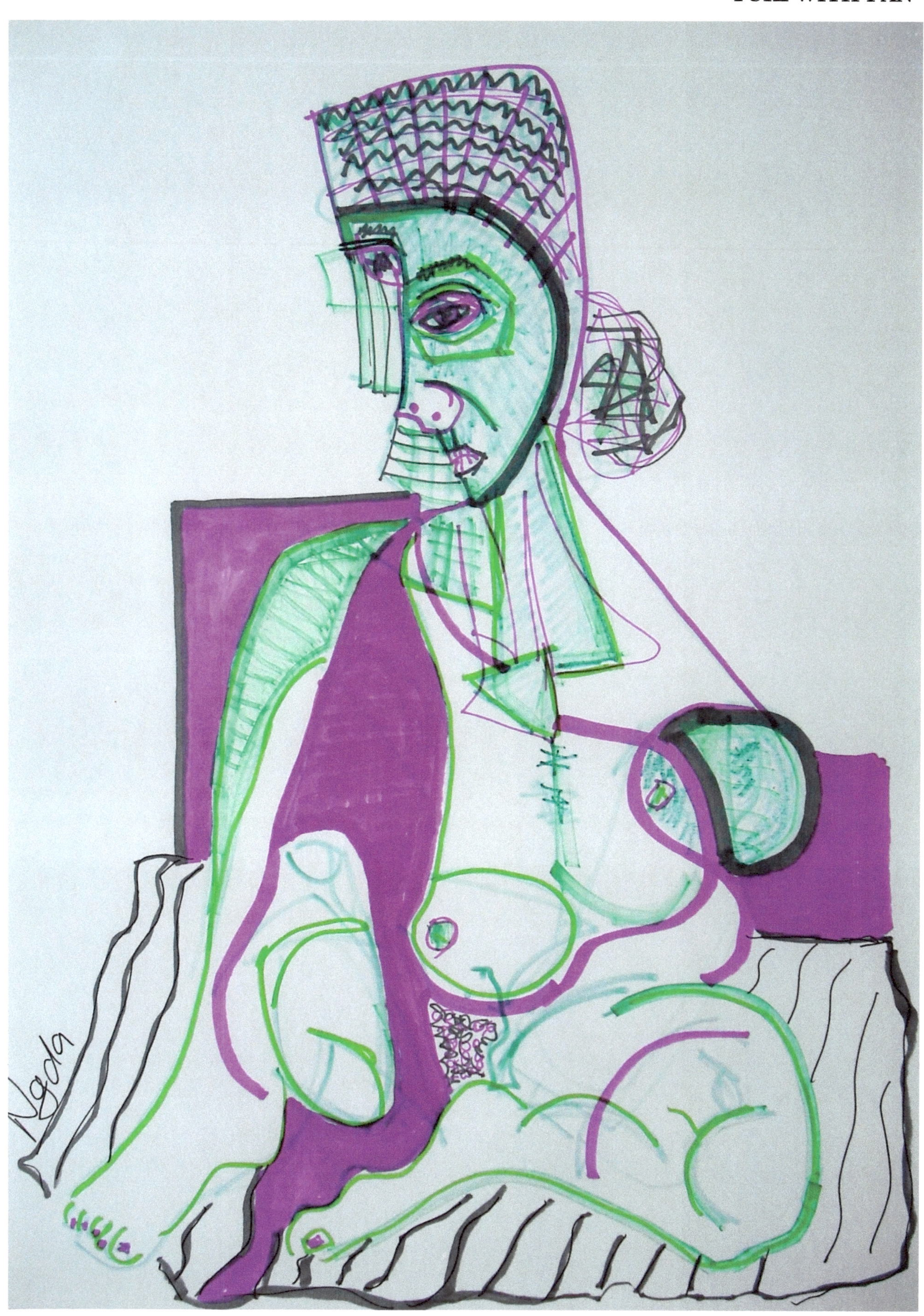

"EVA RESTING"

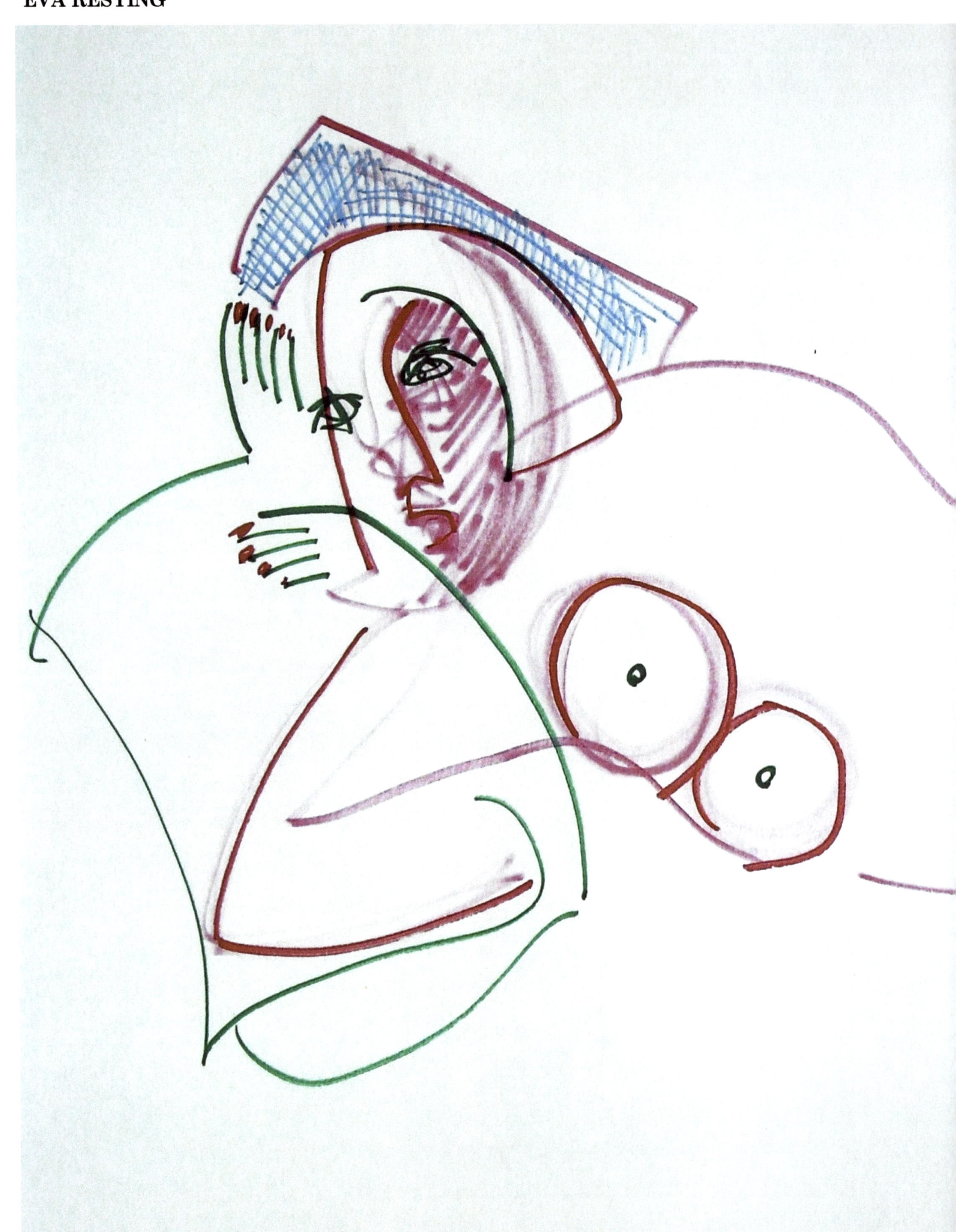

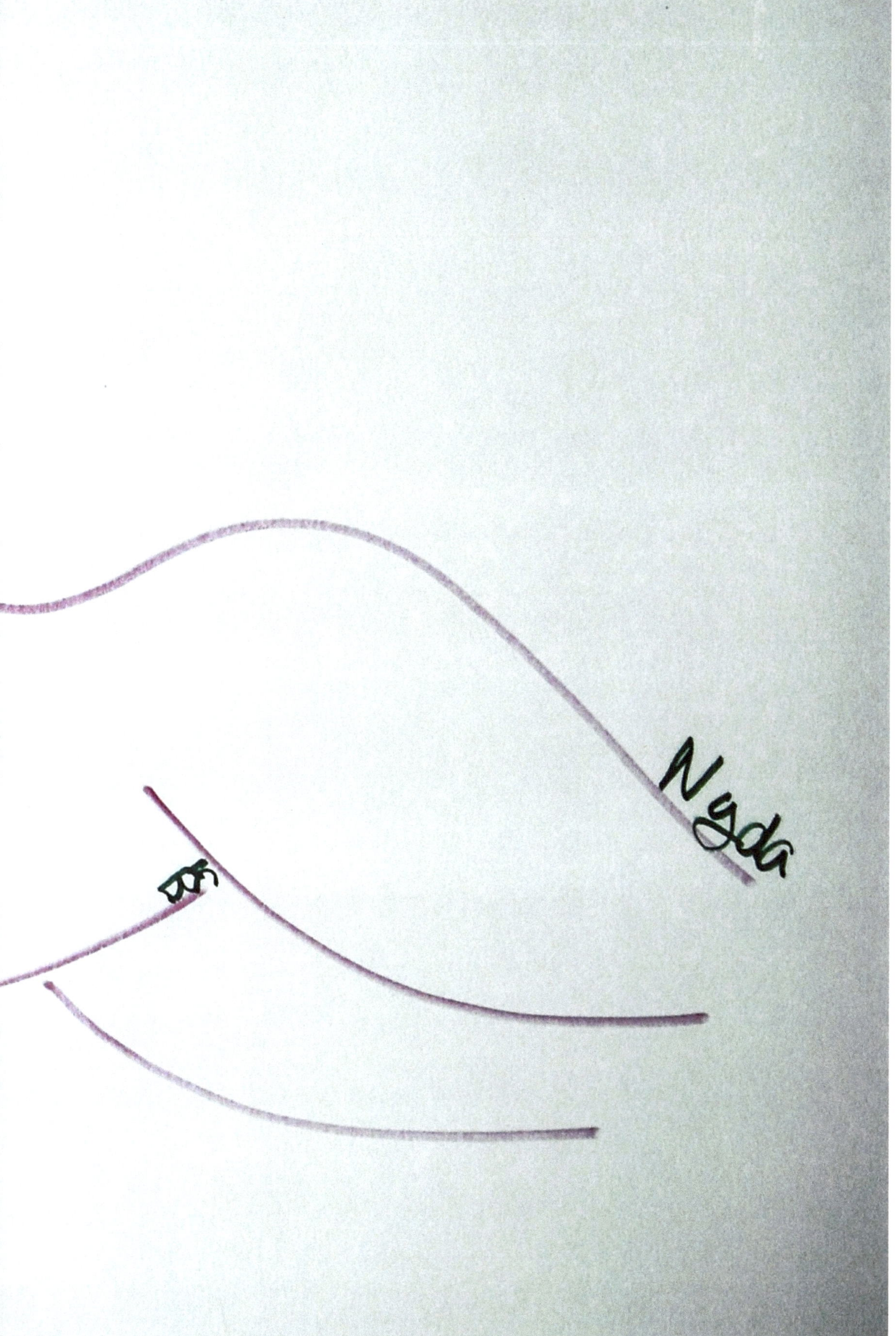
Nyda

"LILIAN AND VEE"

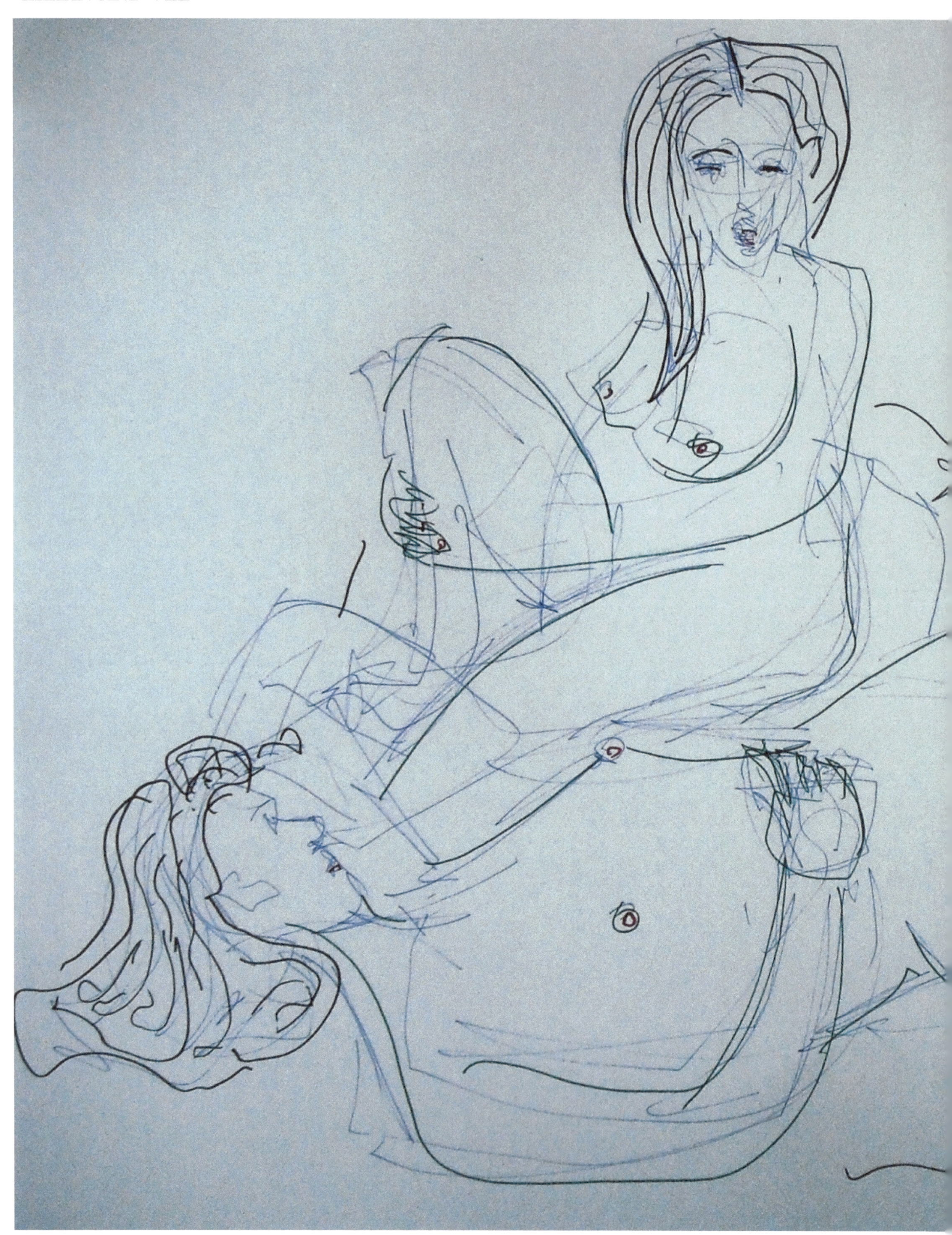

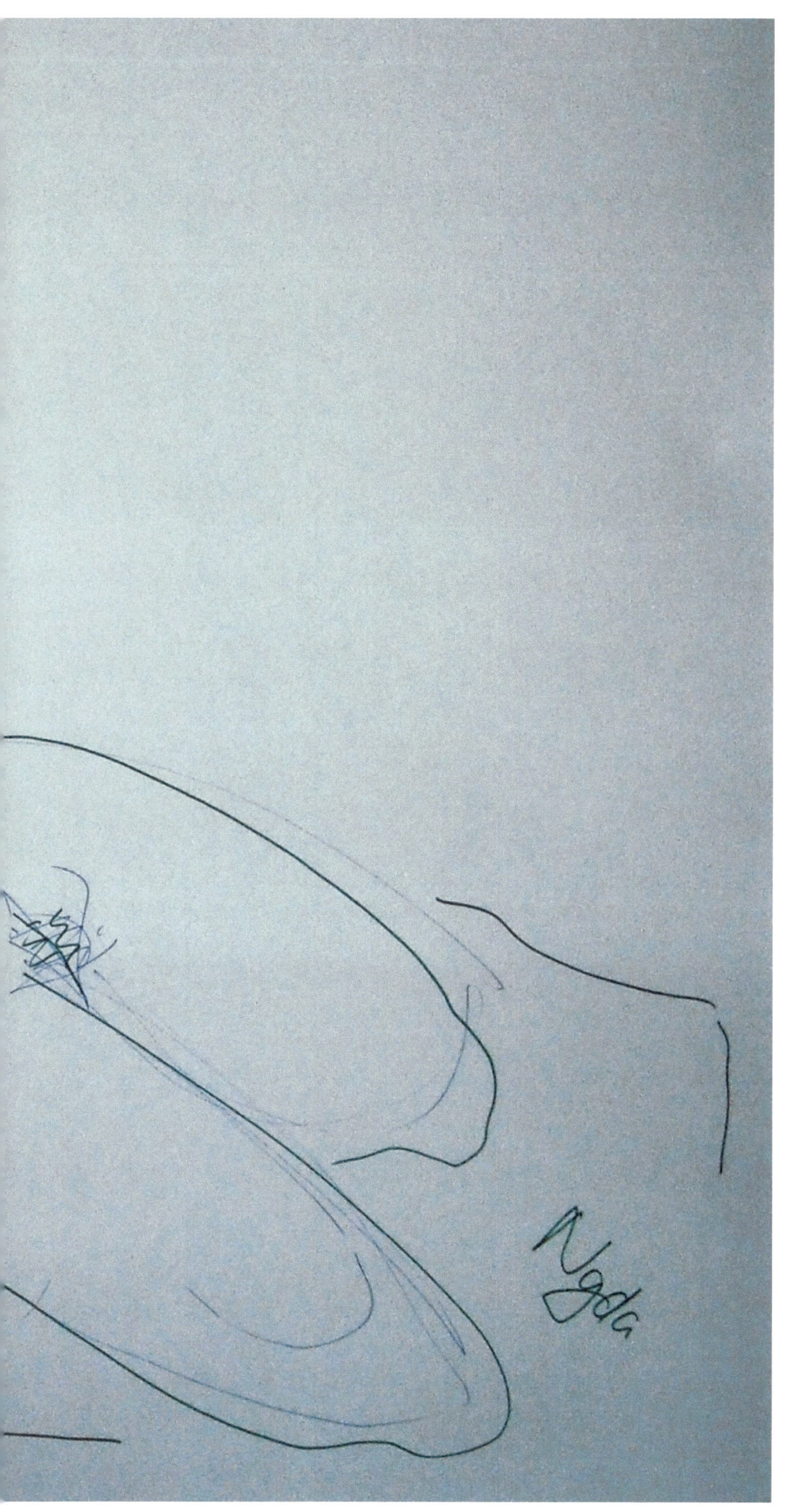

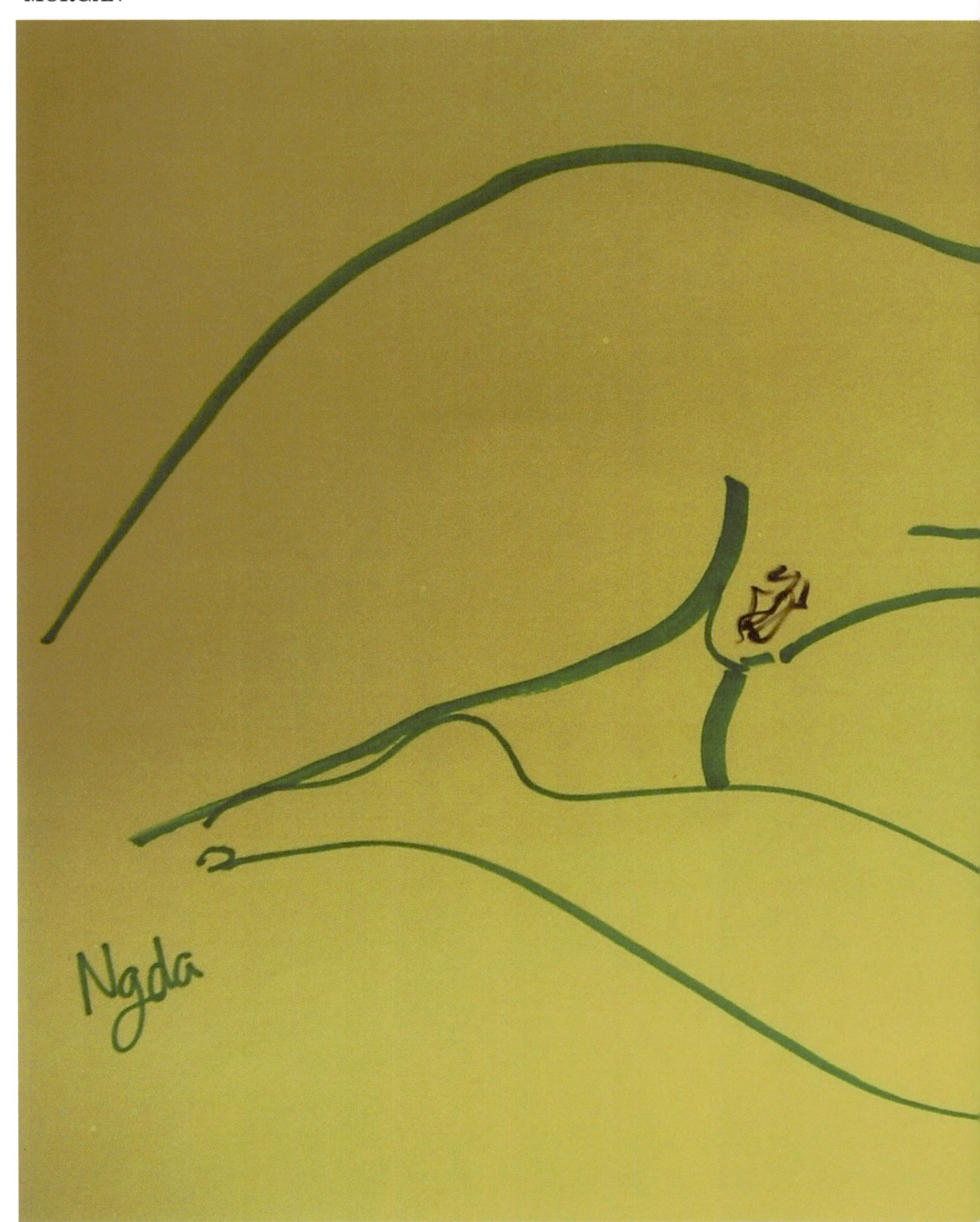

"MORGAN"

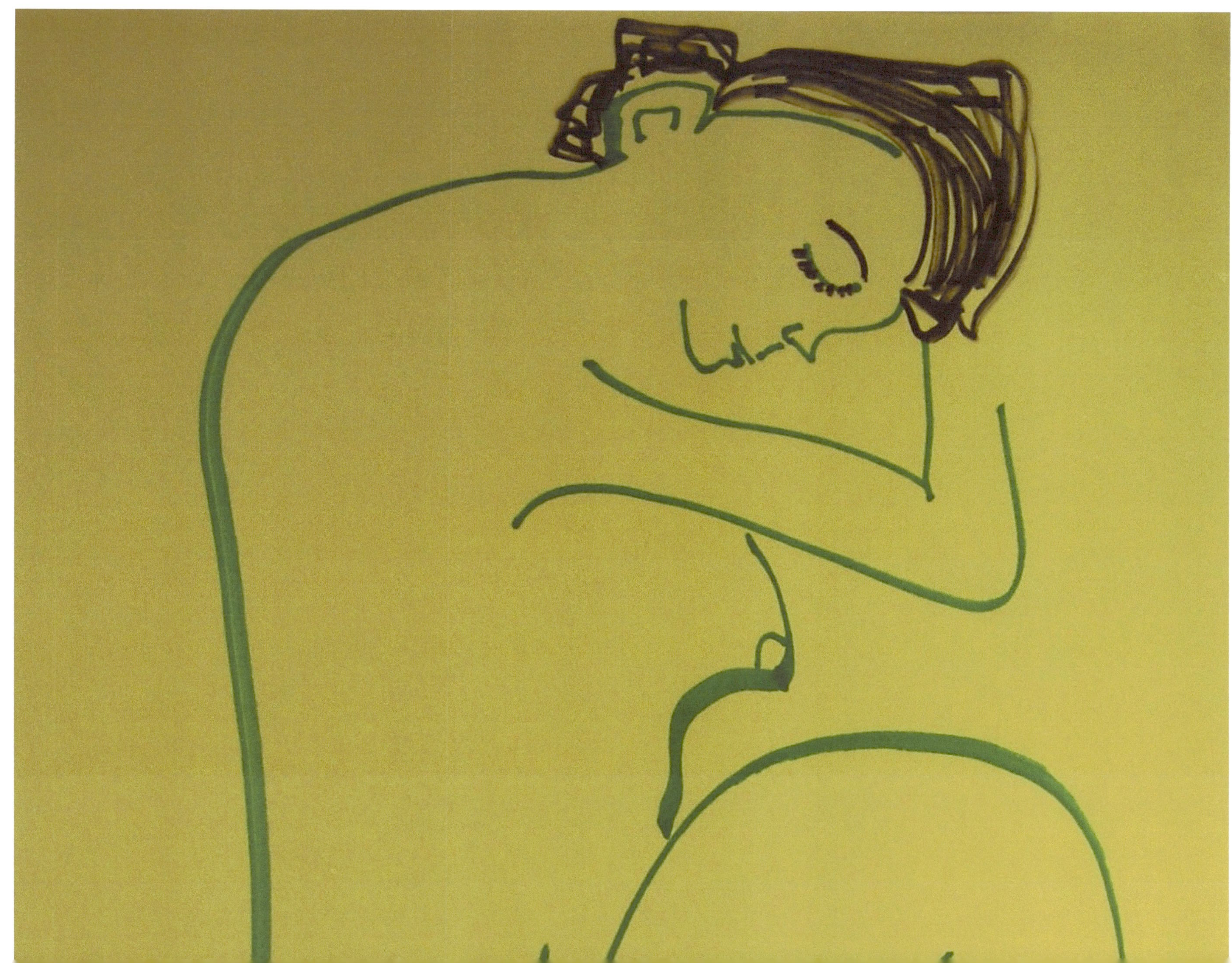

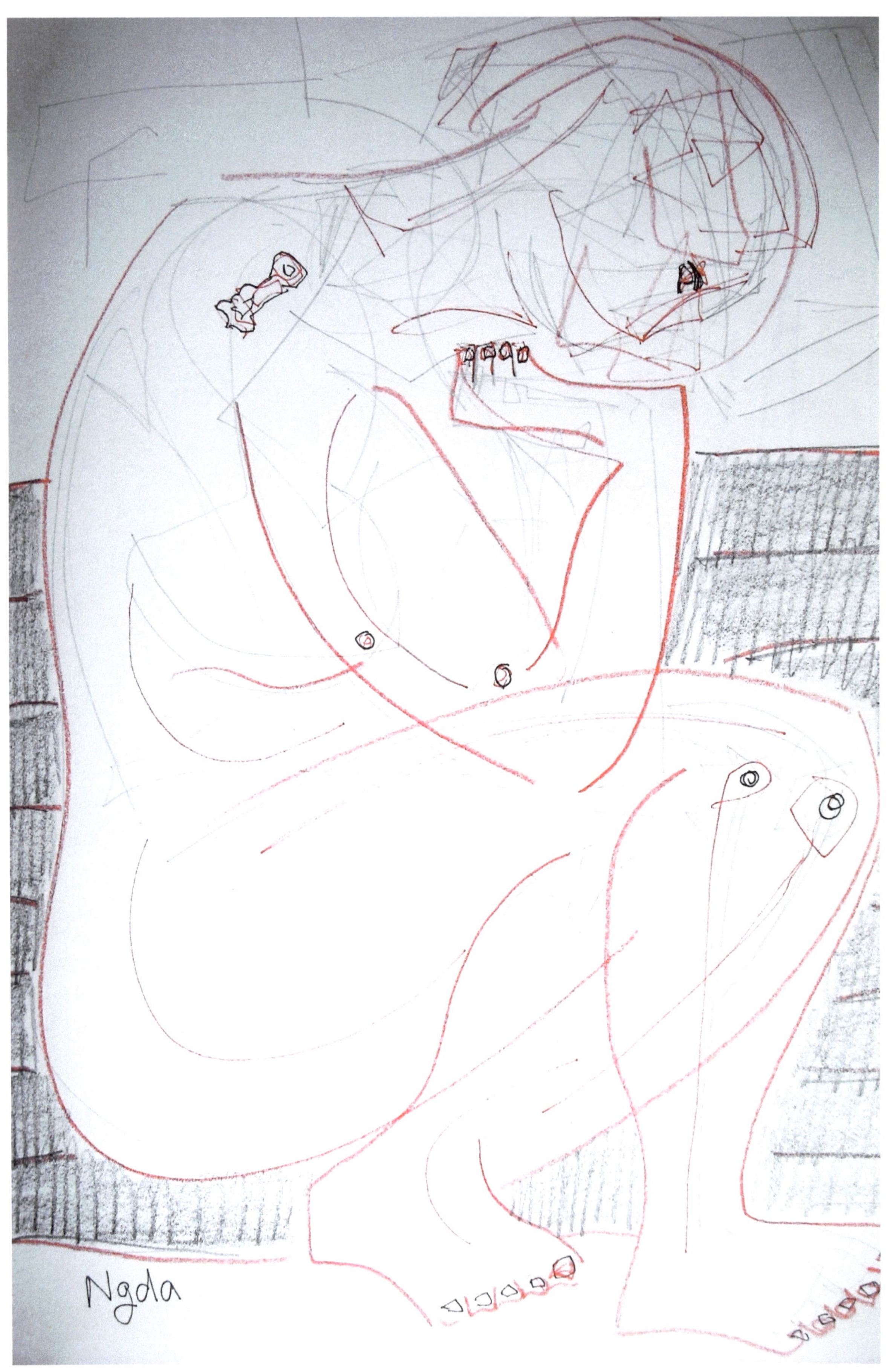
Ngola

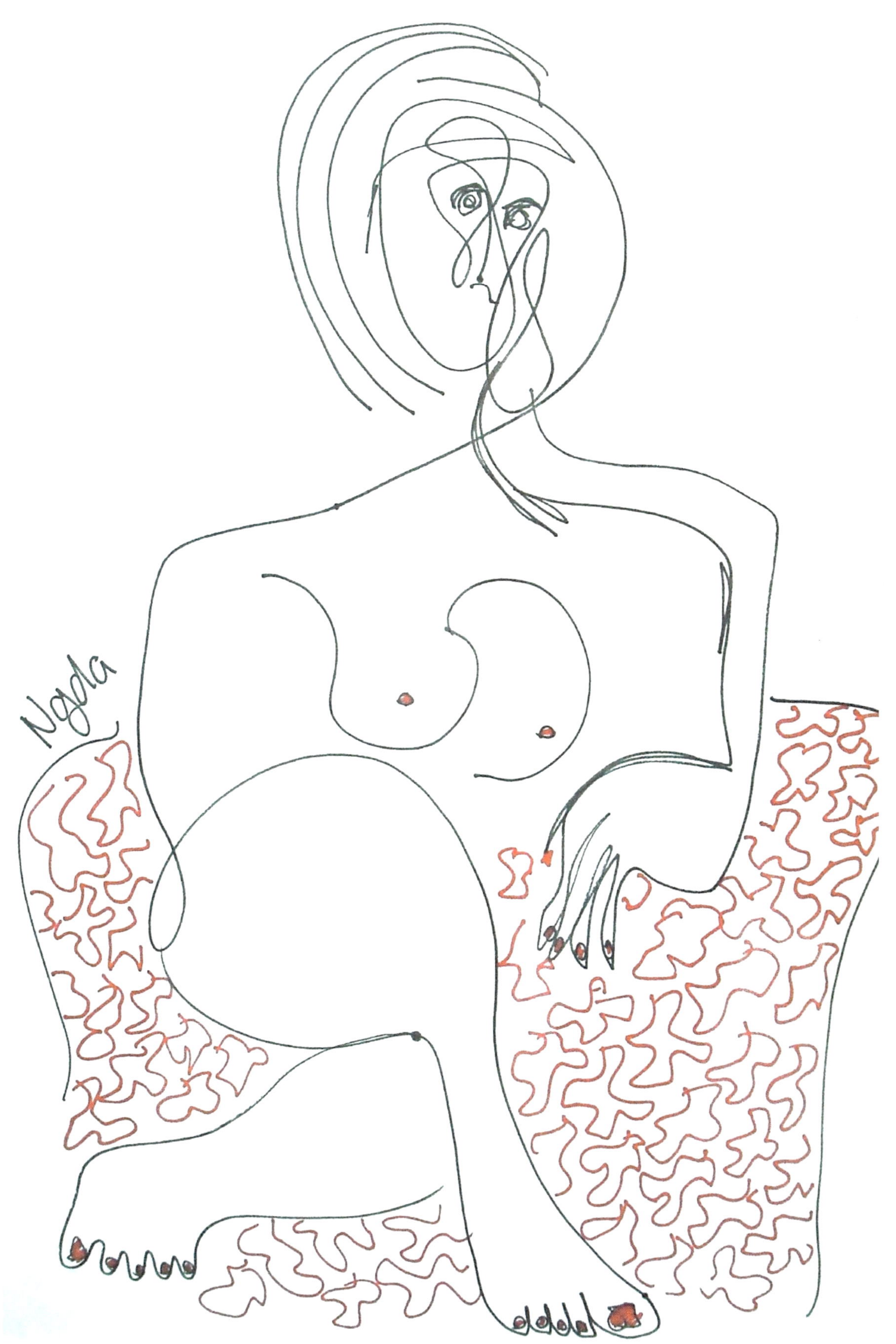

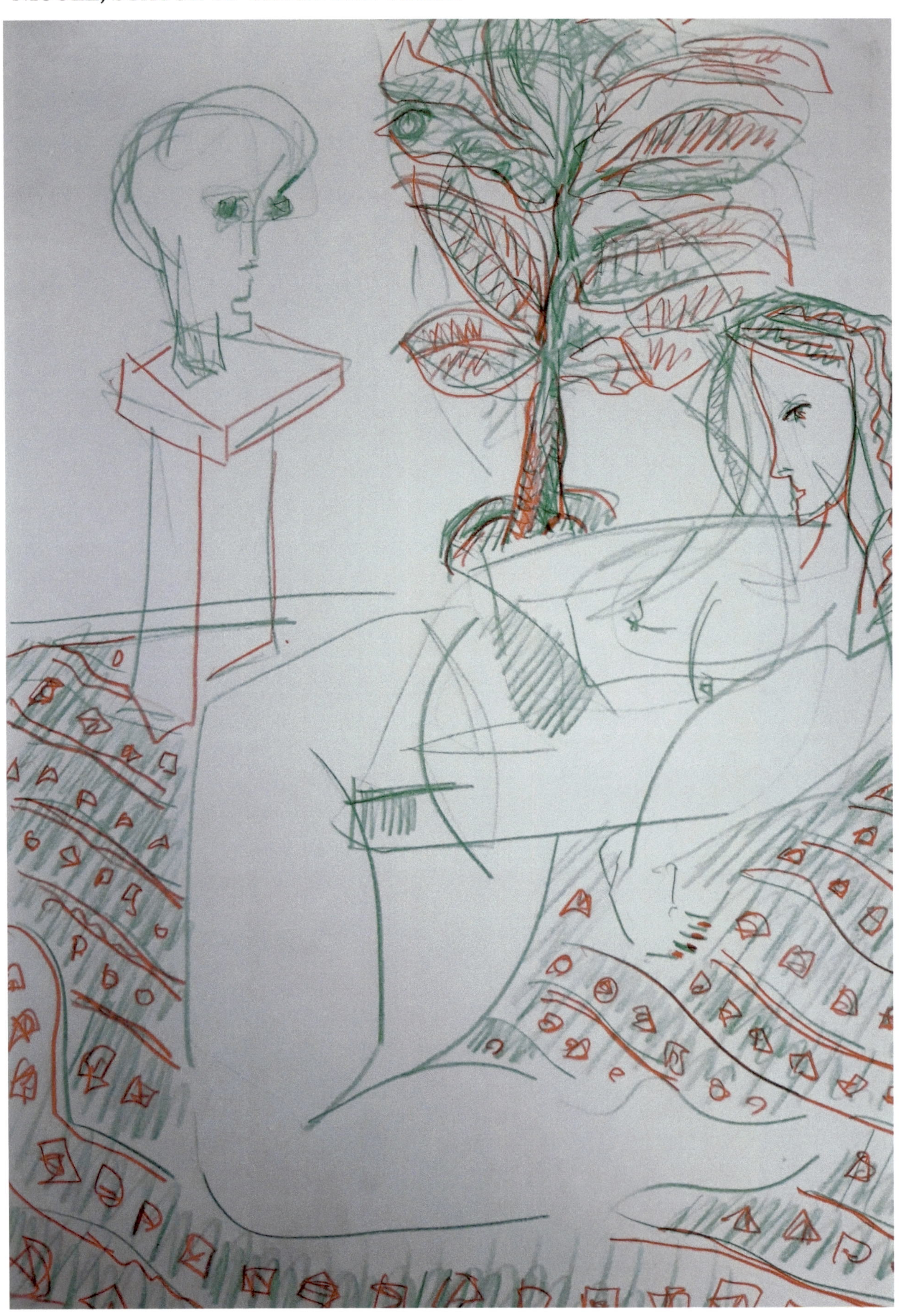

Najda in Line

"This Valley of Tears"

Agora Gallery

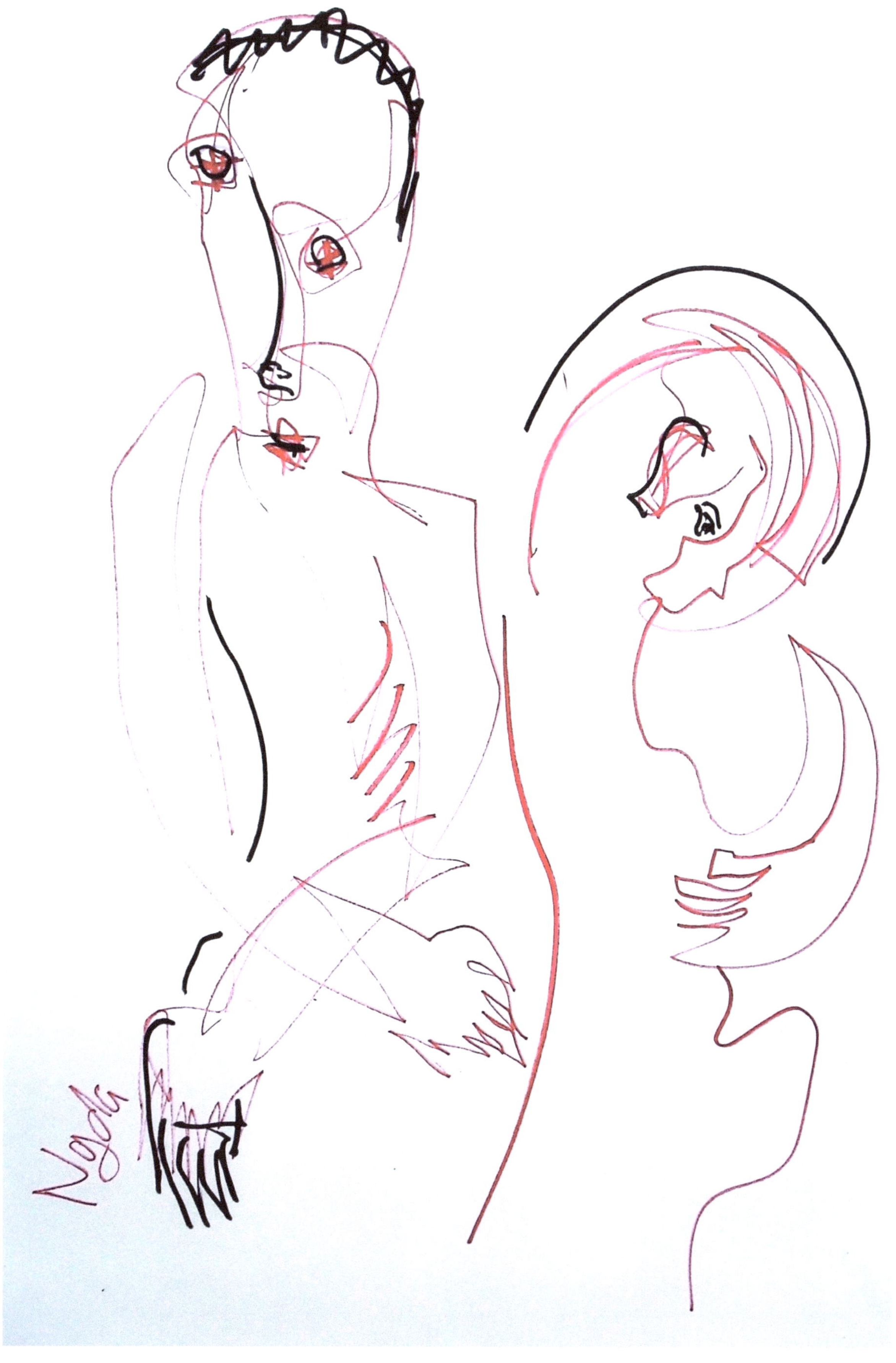

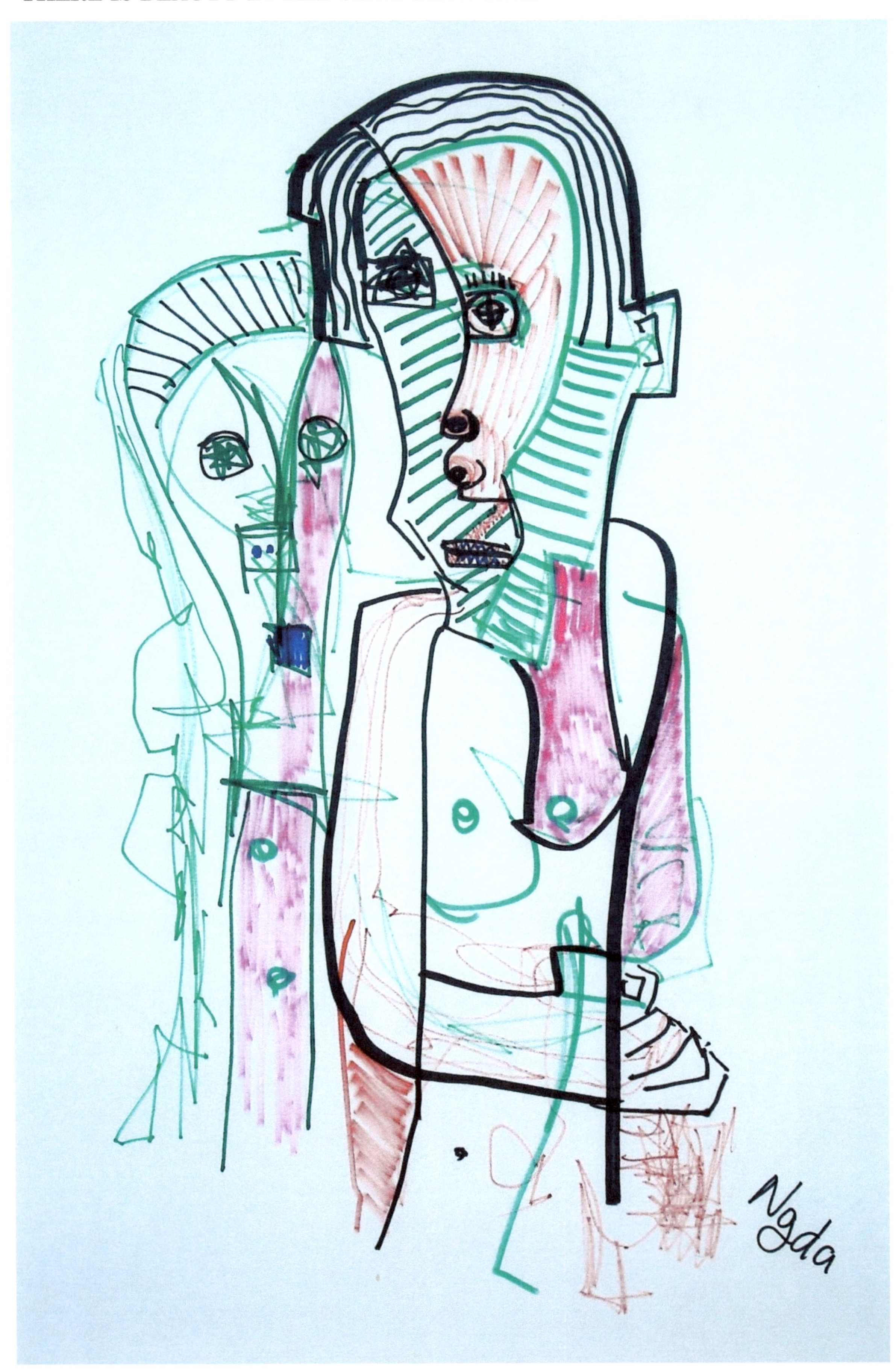

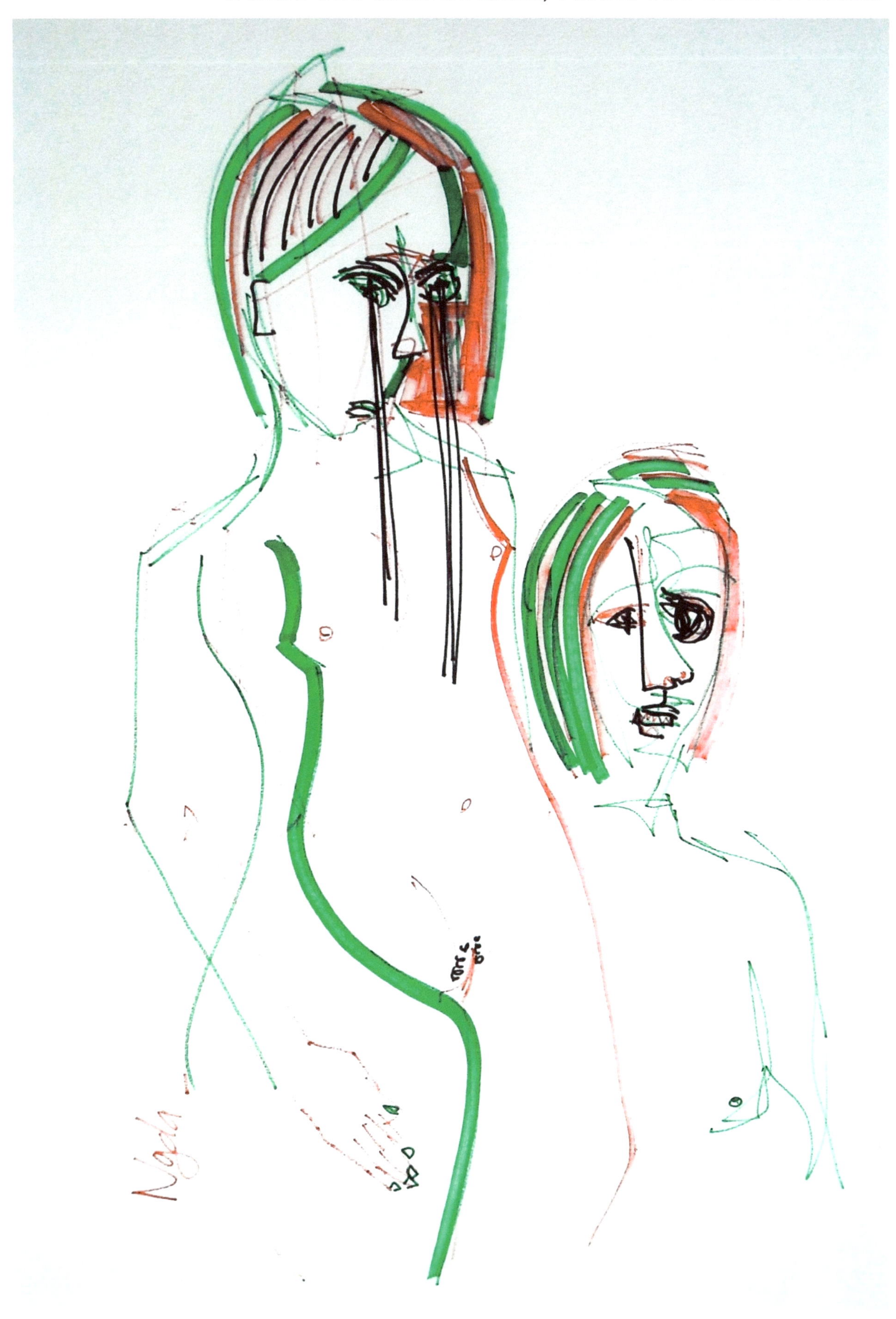

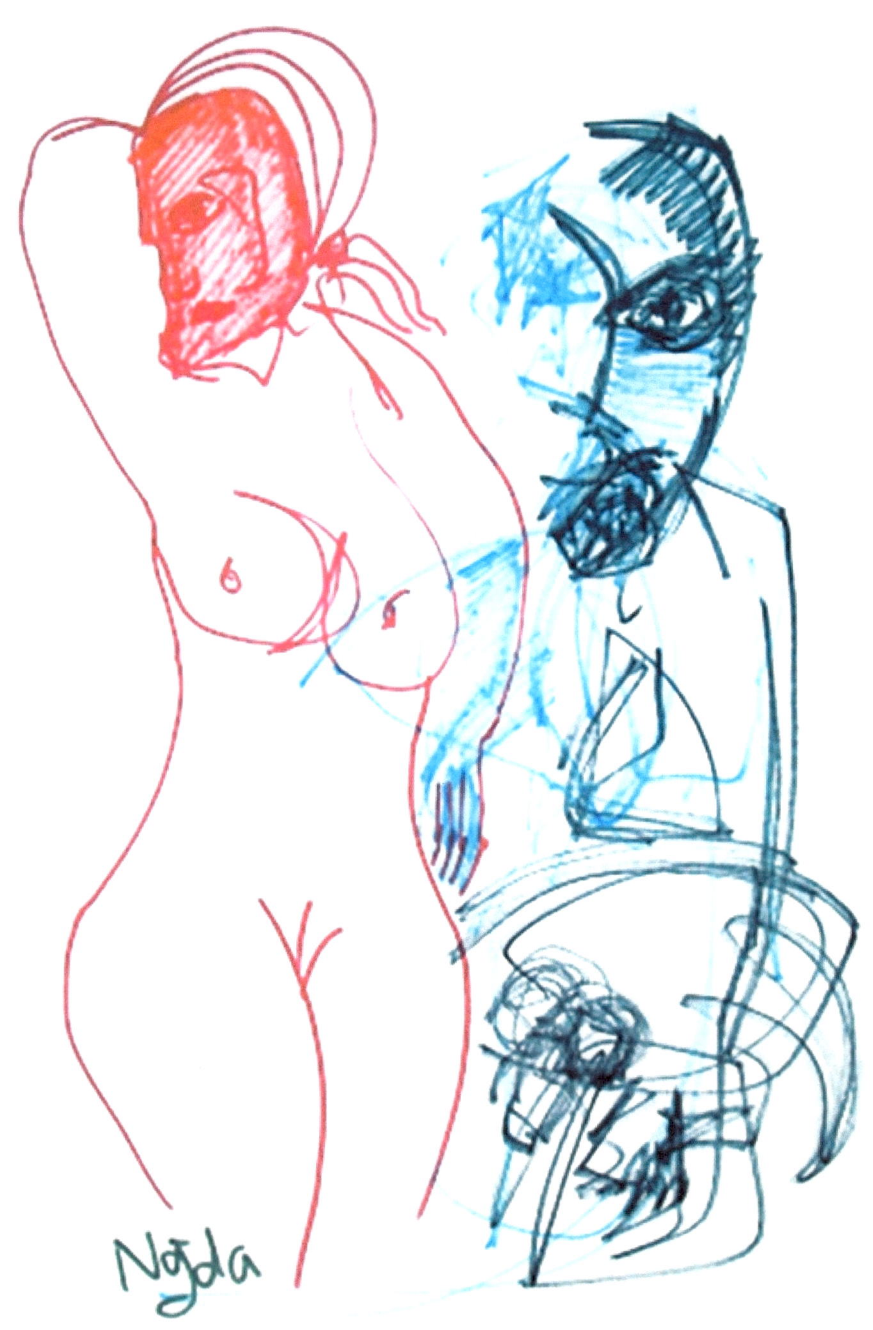

Najda in Line
"INDEX"

INDEX
Najda in Line

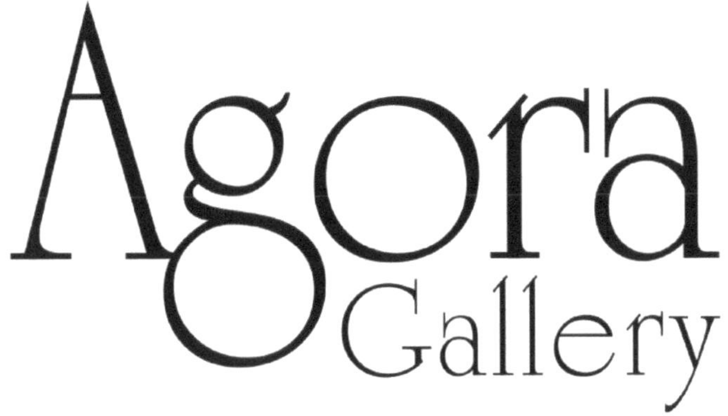

**The artworks were on display at the Agora Gallery
530 W 25th St, Chelsea, New York, USA**

More Artworks by Stephen Najda can be seen:

www.najda.net
Facebook: Najda Art
E-mail enquires: najdaart@gmail.com